democracy squared

a digital revolution that's about to democratise democracy

by Jon Barnes

edited by Jim Ralley

a Flux Publishing book

v1.1

references

References should belong at the front of a book, because without them, nothing that follows would be possible. I hope I've included them all.

Wikipedia, TED, Lawrence Lessig, Matthew Syed, Nassim Taleb, John Buck, Tim Berners-Lee, Yuval Harari, Ricardo Semler, Frederic Laloux, civichouse, The Icelandic Crowdsourced Constitution, Estonian e-Residency, Partido Del Red, Democracy Earth, DemocracyOS, MiVote, Colin Megill, Pol.is, Institute For The Future, ResponsiveOrg (Aaron Dignan, Adam Pisoni, Matthew Partovi, Mike Arauz and Steve Hopkins), Varun Dutt and Cleotilde Gonzalez at Carnegie Mellon, Ray Kurzweil, Gordon Moore, Alvin Toffler, Clayton Christensen, Toyota, D:School, Gerard Endenburg, Audrey Tang, The Noun Project and their contributors Tinashe Mugayi, Tinashe Mugayi, Creative Stall, Hea Poh Lin, Ashwini Sukhdeve, Joao, Lauro Fonte.

contents

flux publishing & the authors

Democracy Squared is the first book published by Flux Publishing. I (Jon) wrote it and Jim edited it.

Flux Publishing is a part of *flux*, which is an organisational evolution studio Jim & I founded dedicated to helping our humanity thrive by liberating organisations for human & commercial benefit. We work with organisations of all shapes and sizes, consulting, advising and coaching them towards organisational methods which are more innovative and more equipped to deal with change and complexity. Here's a little more about us:

jon barnes

For almost 10 years I have been wrestling with concepts and ideas to make organisations places which feel free. Free from power, ego, secrecy and corruption. Free for people to be in charge of their own lives. Free from the waste of resources and human potential which commercially cripples companies.

Born in 1987, I see the internet as the evolutionary platform from which this notion and many other revolutionary changes will happen. These are some of the many concepts that I speak about at conferences, in my work teaching in Exec MBA programmes such as HEC Paris and use to consult businesses with the organisational evolution studio I co-founded, *flux*.

In this book I have put thoughts that have been simmering for a long time. As for for any shortcomings, I'm confident the very smart people I interviewed to create this book will make up for that. I wrote this book in the hope for a more just world. I wish you that too.

jim ralley

For the last few years I've been looking for a way to bring more political, social, and cultural engagement into my work. The beautiful thing about starting your own company is that you get to do whatever you want. So at *flux* we do deep research and publish books alongside consulting with organisations to change the way they work, and growing a network of like-minded partners. This book is Jon's baby. I've done my best to help it flow a bit better, be a little more rigorous, and make sense to people who aren't privy to the inner workings of Jon's brain. It's been so inspiring to meet all of these people doing amazing things with tech to transform democracy. It's radically changed my perspective on what we can all do to make our dent in the universe.

This is just the beginning: education, manufacturing, media, healthcare, etc. There are many big subjects that we'll tackle over the next few years. We exist to liberate people and organisations, from broken workplaces, inadequate schools, and failing democracies. If you're into that too, join us at **flux.am**

This is for everyone.
- Sir Tim Berners-Lee, inventor of the World Wide Web

the call to arms: a revolution with an alternative

This book is intended to be a snapshot in time, because in the time it takes to go to print/eBook, some of the content will already be outdated. And that's part of the story, of a world that is changing, where the very foundations are shaking. This isn't a rigorous and detailed academic textbook on tech democracy and evolutionary theory (you can Google that). This book is meant to offer a provocative perspective. A kind of documentary. A documentary about revolution. Just not the kind of revolution we're used to seeing on TV. No bricks through windows, tear gas being sprayed at kids in hoodies, cars being set alight, police running with shields. This is about changing the deepest, most fundamental and underlying systems of the modern world. This isn't about left and right, democrats and republicans, ins and outs, blacks and whites. This is about creating webs not walls. This is about revolutionising democracy.

In the past 25 years, the internet has changed pretty much everything we know. Almost anybody can become a media mogul. Build a hotel empire. Become an A-List musician. Almost anybody can be almost anything. Except a politician. The internet is often heralded as the great disrupter and democratiser of everything in modern society. Except for one thing: democracy itself.

This book is about revolutionaries around the world who are about to take the establishment by storm. They are taking on the biggest challenge the Internet has faced to date: democratising democracy.

You may not have heard of them all, but they exist. Whether its 'Podemos' in Spain, 'Movimento 5 Stelle' in Italy, the 'NetParty' in Argentina, or the 'Pirate Party' in Iceland, there is a new breed of activists around the world using technology to usher in an era where 'we the people' can be the genuine social contributors we are entitled to be. This revolution promises moral and monetary upheaval. It promises a move from the peaks and troughs of boom and bust economics and a breakaway from divisive propaganda and rhetoric. The professional politician could be about to become another extinct dinosaur that the Internet leaves in its wake.

This is a revolution with the promise of genuine alternatives to a system that has disenfranchised so many. These alternatives use technology to decentralise basic human notions of trust, freedom and equality. They could create a society which constantly iterates on lessons of the past, always evolving the way in which we live together. An alternative which gives minorities a voice. Which improves equality in society. Which is more in-line with our basic human rights.

This book is a story about what I believe will be the most fundamental democratic revolution the world has seen since Versaille in the late 18th century. It's the French Revolution on steroids. The governing of the people by the people. Every good story has its stars, and the stars of this book are five poster projects from five different countries across the world who are offering starting points for a new direction in the way our planet is governed.

I invite you to join this revolution and to give this alternative the energy it deserves so we can democratise democracy and help our humanity thrive by liberating people and nations the world over.

meet the protagonists

The story I will tell of this revolution is grounded in real examples from real projects by real people. They are our protagonists and they are leaders in a growing community of revolutionaries around the world who are using technology to rebuild our democratic structures from the ground level.

This book is structured in four parts. In the first two I will offer my perspective on the attitudinal and systemic shifts which I think create the context for huge social upheaval and which lay the ground for these amazing projects to flourish and change the world. We're not talking iterative little changes to the existing system, we're talking a complete overhaul towards something which belongs to the world of today and tomorrow, not last century. Once I've laid the groundwork for this movement, in part three I'll hand the mic over to the people doing the real work. I interviewed these amazing people and by sharing their stories in their own words I hope to help us all imagine the shifts we can hope for in our lifetimes, leaving a better world to our children. Then, in part four I'll leave you with some of my insights and considerations for the future, based on their inspiring and groundbreaking work.

Just as it is a fallacy of contemporary society to assume that schoolchildren need teachers and employees need managers, it is equally outdated to take for granted the flawed and unquestioned notion that countries need professional politicians. Or at least professional politicians in the way we currently see them. If the industrial educational system or the depressing state of the modern workplace have left you despondent as to the ability of everyday people with huge ideas to change the world from their laptops, I hope to leave you with the proof that this is exactly what is happening in every continent in the world.

So without any further ado, I'd like to introduce you to the stars of the show:

MiVote

A blockchain-enabled digital platform founded by the articulate intellectual and entrepreneurial Adam Jacoby. Through an approach they call 'destinational democracy' MiVote is intending to create the most genuinely democratic political model that exists in the world today.

Icelandic Crowdsourced Constitution

Following the country's financial collapse in 2008, a group of pioneers from the 'Ministry of Ideas' got together to create the world's first ever crowdsourced constitution. I spoke to their CTO Finnur Magnusson.

pol.is & vTaiwan

Created around the time of the Arab Spring & Occupy movements, pol.is is a platform which uses machine learning to be able to scale large conversations so that they are coherent. The platform has been used successfully in Taiwan where it has contributed to changes in laws through a democratic process which has involved large numbers of people.

Democracy Earth & DemocracyOS

Described by Adam Jacoby (MiVote CEO) as *"rockstars in this tech/democracy world"*, I interviewed one of the founders of a platform that puts citizens in charge of the policies. Santiago Siri gave us some amazing thoughts on the future of democracy and how his platform is contributing to reshaping societies.

Estonia e-Residency

Set on creating the country of the future, Estonia now has 10,000 e-residents and is competing with companies around the world in the service it provides to its digital population. Putting into question the very notion of a nation, we spoke to their MD Kaspar Korjus who told me more about his vision for a future with dynamic borders.

prologue: zooming out

In his perspective-altering book about the history and cultural evolution of humankind, '*Sapiens: A Brief History of Humankind*', Yuval Harari ends with a passage about change and revolution. This sets the perfect context in which I'm writing this book.

The revolutions of the last two centuries have been so swift and radical that they have changed the most fundamental characteristic of the social order. Traditionally, the social order was hard and rigid. 'Order' implied stability and continuity. Swift social revolutions were exceptional, and most social transformations resulted from the accumulation of numerous small steps. Humans tended to assume that the social structure was inflexible and eternal. Families and communities might struggle to change their place within the order, but the idea that you could change the fundamental structure of the order was alien. People tended to reconcile themselves to the status quo, declaring that 'this is how it always was, and this is how it always will be'.

Over the last two centuries, the pace of change became so quick that the social order acquired a dynamic and malleable nature. It now exists in a state of permanent flux. When we speak of modern revolutions we tend to think of 1789 (the French Revolution), 1848 (the liberal revolutions) or 1917 (the Russian Revolution). But the fact is that, these days, every year is revolutionary. Today, even a thirty-year-old can honestly tell disbelieving teenagers, 'When I was young, the world was completely different.' The Internet, for example, came into wide usage only in the early 1990s, hardly twenty years ago. Today we cannot imagine the world without it.

Hence any attempt to define the characteristics of modern society is akin to defining the colour of a chameleon. The only characteristic of which we can be certain is the incessant change. People have become used to this, and most of us think about the social order as something flexible, which we can engineer and improve at will.

It's easy to be victims to a system we see as broken. To complain and moan on Facebook and Twitter, or over drinks with our friends. Signing digital petitions is often the closest most of us get to acting on the kind of systemic change we're capable of creating. Our star players will show us just how deep and systemic a change is possible with entrepreneurship and modern technology in the palm of our hands. They are the people engineering and improving society at will. I hope this book brings out the social engineer in all of us.

part 1: context. the madhouse we live in

Nothing has really changed

Meet my grandma. The cutest 94 year-old British woman you'll ever meet. She was born in 1922, 4 years after the First World War, and was 17 when the Second World War started. Her formative years took place before TV, before the European Union, before commercial air travel, before rock and roll. Before pretty much everything I know.

Now meet my little sister. The cutest 24 year old Franco-British girl you'll ever meet (some bias developing here). She is currently travelling the world making a living blogging on her laptop.

My grandma has seen the most rapid social changes the world has ever known, my sister will see far far more. Some theorists we'll meet later believe that we're only just getting started. We could well be at the beginning of a hockey stick-shaped exponential curve. What's to come? Probably driverless cars, commercial space travel, genuine artificial intelligence, and human genome engineering. The future is looking more and more like a mash-up of Skynet and Gattaca.

Decentralisation and the impact of technology

One of the biggest shifts we are seeing is that intelligence is in many ways distributed across the network of the Internet, but power in nation states is still centralised with Central Governments and Central Banks. The idea of huge centralised organisations largely belongs to the old world. Centralisation adds limiting structures, unnecessary bureaucracy, and huge distances between different layers in a hierarchy. These elements all lead to a system that is highly fallible. The recent paradigm shift in decentralised and distributed systems means that we can move away from this, and towards flatter, more stable structures. In fact, in some circles, the idea of anything centralised is even seen as highly dangerous and irresponsible on a purely pragmatic basis.

Here's an example from outside of government. In information technology, the idea of centralisation creates what is know as a 'single point of failure'. A single point of failure (from Wikipedia) *"is a part of a system that, if it fails, will stop the entire system from working. SPOFs are undesirable in any system with a goal of high availability or reliability, be it a business practice, software application, or other industrial system."* This is why businesses often diversify their revenue and business models, so if one domino falls, the others don't all come toppling down too.

Centralised IT system

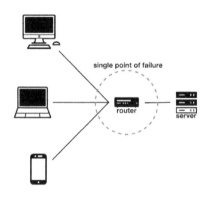

Decentralised IT system

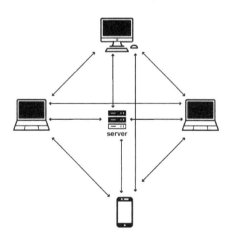

Decentralised systems tend to be faster moving, faster at reaching mass adoption, and faster at constantly improving through iteration. They are far less volatile as there is no single point of failure. The open source movement is a perfect example of this. Take Linus Torvald's Linux operating system for example. It is on more computer hardware platforms than any other operating system in the world. It powers more mobile phones that any other OS, through Google's 'forked' version called Android. Mad, the idea that a non-commercial, freely available piece of work can become one of the world leaders in a market dominated by huge corporations like Apple, Google and Facebook.

Another wonderful example of what decentralisation can do is Wikipedia. In its beginnings there were lots of sceptics, with many saying that the information on the site wasn't accurate enough, and that it was too easily corruptible. Over time though, after 856,348,704 article edits (in just the English language version), Jimmy Wales and the 29,422,514 contributors to the Wikipedia project and have rapidly created the broadest and deepest collection of knowledge that the world has ever known. Wikipedia is the poster child for open source in the digital age. It makes tangible the notion that 'knowledge and truth' are dynamic concepts, always being iterated and improved upon. It makes tangible the concept that collective intelligence can create unbelievable results. And it makes tangible the idea that many people want to contribute to something bigger than themselves.

There are plenty more other examples. Crowdsourcing is an obvious one. Kickstarter has received more than $1.9 billion in pledges from 9.4 million backers to fund 257,000 creative projects. What MySpace did for independent musicians all those years ago, crowdfunding websites do for entrepreneurs. It makes possible for the many what previously was only possible for the few. It means that ideas can be tested and gather momentum without having to rely on funding from friends in high places. It is a wonderful thing for innovation and for unleashing all the latent potential in people. A vehicle for creativity to explode and value to be generated with an in-built culture of meritocracy and crowd validation.

However, the effects of this are yet to be seen in politics on a huge scale. But this is a necessary evolution if we are to move beyond the nonsense of modern political propaganda, exerted by candidates and backed by secret millionaires. In his seminal TED Talk 'We the People, and the Republic we must reclaim', the Harvard Law Professor and democratic thinker Lawrence Lessig goes deep on this point:

The United States (...) has two elections, one we call the general election, the second we should call the money election. In the general election, it's the citizens who get to vote, if you're over 18, in some states if you have an ID. In the money election, it's the funders who get to vote. The trick is, to run in the general election, you must do extremely well in the money election. You don't necessarily have to win. But you must do extremely well. And here's the key: there are few relevant funders in USA-land.

Now you say, really? Really 0.05 percent? Well, here are the numbers from 2010: 0.26 percent of America gave 200 dollars or more to any federal candidate, 0.05 percent gave the maximum amount to any federal candidate, 0.01 percent — the one percent of the one percent — gave 10,000 dollars or more to federal candidates, and in this election cycle, my favorite statistic is .000042 percent — for those of you doing the numbers, you know that's 132 Americans — gave 60 percent of the Super PAC money spent in the cycle we have just seen ending. So I'm just a lawyer, I look at this range of numbers, and I say it's fair for me to say it's 0.05 percent who are our relevant funders in America.

Now, what can we say about this democracy in

USA-land? Well, as the Supreme Court said in 'Citizens United', we could say, of course the people have the ultimate influence over the elected officials. We have a general election, but only after the funders have had their way with the candidates who wish to run in that general election. And number two, obviously, this dependence upon the funders produces a subtle, understated, camouflaged bending to keep the funders happy. Candidates for Congress and members of Congress spend between 30 and 70 percent of their time raising money to get back to Congress or to get their party back into power.

In the USA, 0.05% are deciding on the small group of candidates that 'we the people' get to pick from. Later we will dispute whether there is even a need anymore to be voting for representatives in the first place, but for now, assuming we do need them, it is nowhere near democratic for 99.95% of the population to have to pick from the teachers' pets of the 0.05%.

Crowdfunding could be the answer to this. Rather than 'few giving lots', 'many could give little'. A dollar vote kind of thing. Then more people would be able to be elected if their story was compelling enough. This isn't to say we wouldn't still suffer from the other vast social inequalities that exist, but it would certainly be better than the oligarchic democracy we're working from today.

And this is the kind of lens I would like to see this book through. One which shows that a total restructuring from a totally different perspective is needed. It's not about who gets elected, it's about how we make our choices.

Anyway, back to money. Of course, we couldn't open up a discussion about distributed financial systems, without mentioning Bitcoin and the blockchain it is built on. The World Economic Forum believes that by 2027, 10% of GDP will be stored on blockchain-related technology. Wikipedia of course captures and explains Bitcoin succinctly (thanks Jimmy et al):

> *The system works without a central repository or single administrator, the U.S. Treasury categorizes bitcoin as a decentralized virtual currency. Bitcoin is often called the first cryptocurrency, although prior systems existed and it is more correctly described as the first decentralized digital currency. Bitcoin is the largest of its kind in terms of total market value.*

For many people, it isn't Bitcoin that is necessarily interesting, but the peer-to-peer technology it works on known as 'the blockchain'. Many people reading this will understand far more than I do about the blockchain. Here is how the 'Institute For The Future' explain the blockchain in simple terms:

> *When you vote have you ever wondered if your ballot is actually counted?! When you meet somebody online, how do you know they're who they say they are?! When you buy coffee that's labeled fair-trade, what makes you so certain of its origin?!*

> *To be sure, really sure about any of those questions, you'd need a system where records could be stored, facts could be verified by anyone and security is guaranteed that way nobody could cheat the system by editing records because everybody using the system would be watching.*

> *Systems like this are on the horizon and the software that powers them is called a blockchain. Blockchains store information across a network of personal computers, making them not just decentralised but distributed. This means no central company or person owns the system, yet everyone can use it and help run it. This is important because it means it's difficult for any one*

person to take down the network or corrupt it. The people who run the system use their computers to hold bundles of records submitted by others, known as "blocks", in a chronological chain. The blockchain uses a form of math called cryptography to ensure that records can't be counterfeited or changed by anyone else.

You've probably heard of the blockchain's first killer app. A form of digital cash called Bitcoin that you can send to anyone, even a complete stranger. Bitcoin is different from credit cards, PayPal or other ways to send money because there isn't a bank or financial middleman involved. Instead people around the world help move the money around by validating others' Bitcoin transactions with their personal computers, earning a small fee in the process. Bitcoin uses the blockchain by tracking records of ownership over the digital cash, so only one person can be the owner at a time and the cash can't be spent twice, like counterfeit money in the physical world can.

This is only the beginning. In the future the blockchain could enable us to launch companies that are entirely run by algorithms, making self-driving cars safer, help us protect our online identities, and even track the billions of devices on the internet of things. These innovations will change our lives forever and it's just the beginning.

If we move beyond money, this also means that using this technology we can create virtual voting systems. The fear for many people I speak to about online voting systems, is the potential for fraud. But as you can see with blockchain, this isn't necessarily the case preventing the system from being hacked and people from copy and pasting votes.

The impact of this could be enormous, allowing many more people to vote much more often on more direct things. This is already being used in several examples of progressive digital direct democracy, which we will examine later when we meet the people behind these projects.

Not to get too philosophical here, but this can all be explained if we look at the nature of our transactions a little more and the belief systems which underpin them. The reason we have central banks and financial institutions is because we place our trust in them. Millions of people trust banks with millions of dollars every day. It's all about trust. What the blockchain does is decentralise and distribute the notion of trust itself.

This can apply to pretty much anything. I trust the polling station with my vote but if we decentralise that notion, we would distribute trust amongst the many. The risk attached to corruption and wrongdoing also gets distributed with the trust we put in the blockchain, thus making it less susceptible to malicious practices.

This idea of decentralising trust is possibly one of the biggest shifts we're having to deal with as a society. It is one of the reasons why so many businesses resist change, and why some people resist technology. Not because of the technology itself but because it is messing with our inherited beliefs that trust is something you put in one central place or institution rather than spreading it across a network. This is something some industries get and some don't, as we're about to see.

There are of course plenty of commercial examples of decentralised systems disrupting established business models and industries. Like Uber creating a trusted, global, decentralised system for users to access transportation services to get people and things from A to B. Or Airbnb creating a similarly decentralised platform for people to access accommodation anywhere in the world, in a way that is cheaper, faster, easier, and has more choice than the old hotel industry can possibly deliver. Of course, these organisations aren't saints either and whilst the platform democratises a lot of value creation for people, there are also a number of allegations of exploitative working practices from the platform owners.

These services too, could of course be distributed. If we go to the end of decentralisation principles, the platform cooperativism movement shows how this could work. Neal Gorenflo, the founder of Shareable, an award-winning nonprofit news, action and connection hub for the sharing transformation asks, *"What if Uber was owned and governed by its drivers? What if Airbnb was owned and governed by its hosts?"* This is starting to happen with companies like Fairmondo, co-operative version of eBay, where sellers on the platform are also its owners. Or Stocksy, a stock photo site where the photographers are the owners. Or the driver-owned taxi cooperative Union Taxi in Denver, Colorado.

Other possibly more radical decentralised technologies are still in their infancy and could see a whole wave of old centralised systems falling. Mesh networking is just one example. We now live in a world where there are far more mobile devices than humans. Mobile data traffic has grown 400-million-fold over the past 15 years. The trend is moving inexorably towards total global mobile adoption in the next few years, in the same way that cars (a relatively modern technology) reached mass adoption over the last 100 years. So in a world where everyone has a mobile phone, everyone now has a device that can broadcast and receive data. Mesh networking allows devices to communicate with one another without the need for a centralised transmitter. In the near future we may not need Vodafone, China Mobile, AT&T, or Verizon to manage our communications. The global network of smart devices will do it for you. Firechat is a tangible example of mesh networking. A messaging app for mobile devices that works without the need for internet access or cellular data. It's already been used for mass communication in situations where that communication is absolutely essential, to help people in natural disaster areas, and to power revolutions (from http://www.opengarden.com/firechat):

> *- Natural disasters including floods in Kashmir (April 2015) and Chennai (October 2015), the eruption of volcano Cotopaxi in Ecuador (August 2015), and hurricane Patricia in Mexico (October 2015).*
> *- Massive events: pro-democracy protests in Taiwan (April 2014), Hong Kong (September 2014), the Bersih anti-corruption movement in Malaysia (August 2015), and the visit of the Pope in the Philippines (January 2015).*
> *- Historical elections in Venezuela (December 2015) and the Republic of the Congo (March 2016).*

- Large festivals in India, Canada and the US, including Burning Man

So if the previous examples of distributed systems could predict the fall of central banks, investment banks, universities, hotel chains, and taxi companies, we could very soon be adding telecoms companies to this list. That's 100,000s of jobs gone as soon as something like Firechat reaches mass adoption, and whilst that feels far away, adoption of digital technologies is often exponential which is why we're always surprised when stuff gets big, fast. WhatsApp now has a userbase of 1 billion, just 6 years after launch, and it's basically rendered the SMS market for telcos utterly redundant. Skype did exactly the same with long-distance phone calls 13 years ago.

I don't know what will happen in the future, other than it seems pretty clear that we are operating according to new principles. Principles which are probably only in their very early stages and are yet to reach their full potential. In this book I'm exploring how these principles will redefine the way we govern ourselves.

From hierarchies to #hashtags

So I don't know if the world is better or worse than before, but it's definitely different and it's getting more and more different more and more quickly. Furthermore, it's not just different on the surface, in the things we consume, the clothes we wear, and the entertainment we watch. It's fundamentally different in how humanity is organised, how power is distributed, how we interact, and how information is shared. We now have the evolutionary context to genuinely move from slow, centralised hierarchies to fast, decentralised networks: or as I like to say from *hierarchies to hashtags*.

This shift is deeply disruptive, not only because of the effect it has on businesses in all industries, or on job markets, but also because it puts into question our deep, fundamental human needs. It puts into question the unspoken social norms which still dictate our day to day lives. We may have shifted almost completely from monarchies and dictators to elected governments, but the underlying assumptions around 'how government and democracy works' have not shifted that much. Power being held by the few is still a given in the social fabric of the past century. The legal, political and organisational systems we are living in were created for a world that is rapidly becoming obsolete.

The technological era we find ourselves in allows for a genuine alternative to this. This era provides a context where we should no longer only get to vote for a narrow pool of electoral candidates who may or may not broadly represent our political views. A context where we should no longer be at the whim of a privileged, power-hungry, professional elite. Or at least a context where we can have more influence over how things are decided by those in power. The technology exists to enable everybody to contribute to deciding 'how we decide'. I believe there is a true power shift happening in the world. That shift is one from 'powerful people' to 'powerful processes'. Highly participative processes, where everyone is equally powerful.

Distributing power is a very scary thing to some people. And perhaps justifiably so. How can the crowd be trusted? What if it takes us in a direction that harms us? Are the people educated and informed enough to make the right choices? I think there is equal cause to focus on the opportunities that distribution and the decentralisation of power offers us, to create the kind of society we would like to live in. Over the course of this book, when these kinds of questions pop up, I invite you to ask yourself whether the current system is actually any better than the one we're exploring here. Whether what this book proposes is any worse than what exists already. In my mind, what we have at the moment is pretty terrible. A world run by professional politicians with little experience in the various areas they have mandate and power over.

The system in most countries has gone largely unchanged since the 18th century. Of course there have been numerous changes in policy and in people, but the fundamental operating system is pretty much the same. It's like politics is still punching in rudimentary commands on MS-DOS whilst the rest of the planet is walking around with powerful machines in their pockets. Time for an upgrade.

The hotter it gets, the hotter it gets: the need for speed

The shift I've started describing is well documented and obvious to many. What is sometimes less evident is the extent to which this is alien in respect to how many people think. The impact of this decentralisation is systemic. What do I mean by systemic? Here is a quote by John Buck from his 2007 book *'We The People: Consenting To A Deeper Democracy'*. We will refer back to his work again later, but here he describes the potential impacts of what is popularly known as Systems Thinking:

> *In an open system of interconnected parts, small events can cause large changes and a change in one area can adversely affect another area. A system is a dynamic and complex whole that interacts as a structured functional unit. It may be composed of parts seeking equilibrium but can also exhibit chaotic or exponential growth or decay.*

Whilst this may seem obvious, considering popular expressions like the 'butterfly effect' or the 'domino effect', this way of thinking goes totally against the way we normally see the world. We human beings tend to see trends and trajectories in what is often termed as a 'linear way of thinking'. We see things in sequences, in orders, in simplistic cause and effect terms. This is a trick of the mind which is a fundamental misunderstanding of the world around us. We have difficulties seeing changes in the world from both a zoomed-in and zoomed-out perspective. Time and time again we get tricked by the exponential change that surrounds us. Let us explore a few examples of this phenomenon.

Global warming

This tendency to think in a linear fashion is particularly evidenced by the fact that we seem to be surprised by big events regularly, events which we either didn't foresee happening so quickly, or which we thought were just fads. A simple metaphor for this is the parable of the boiled frog. It is said that if you drop a frog into boiling hot water, the frog will jump out immediately from the shock. However, if you drop a frog into room temperature water and gradually increase the temperature to boiling point, the frog will not notice the subtle increase and will die in the pan. Whether this is true or not, it's a neat analogy for global warming. It seems the human race could well be that frog, and our boiling pot is our own planet. Research at Carnegie Mellon by Varun Dutt and Cleotilde Gonzalez exemplifies how seeing the planet's increase in temperature in linear terms leads us to underestimate the threat the planet is under. In their words:

In the case of the earth's climate, people may underestimate the extent of the nonlinear increase in CO2 accumulation. That is because the shape of CO2 emissions has been increasing roughly linearly over time, and people might think that the accumulation will also increase linearly. In practice, an assumption of linear increase will underestimate the actual increase. Furthermore, such underestimations could undermine the urgency of the climate problem and encourage deferment of human actions, leading to wait-and-see behavior.

In the case of climate change this is because we compute this increase through mathematical addition, with the planet warming up by x°C per year:

Linear thinking = planet temperature + x °C + x °C + x °C

In reality, due to the accumulation of CO2 and its amplification effect, the increase in temperature is exponential and therefore should be computed through multiplication. There is a year-on-year amplification of the problem here shown as *y*:

Exponential thinking = planet temperature + (x °C)*y

We can see this compounding effect in this graph from NASA illustrating the increase in

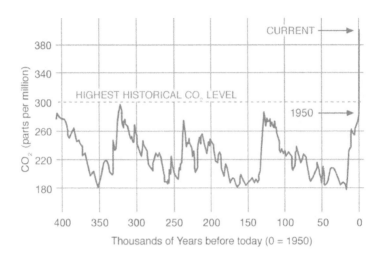

- from climate.nasa.gov

Looking at the sudden exponential increase in the planet's temperature, it's not surprising our minds can't quite get to grips with just how quickly things speed up.

From + to X:
addition to multiplication

So we think the world is changing at a pace of 'a + a + a + a', when in reality it is changing at a pace of 'a x a x a x a'. The speed of change is multiplying, not adding.

To illustrate this difference in the way we think, I sometimes poll audiences when I speak at conferences. I ask them:

> *If company X's revenue was $2million in year 1 and $4million in year 2, what was their revenue in year 3?*

The answers from the audience tend to vary depending on whether their instincts are linear, mildly exponential, highly exponential or radically exponential. The most common answers tend to be 6 and 8. Sometimes you get a 16 but never have I heard somebody assume higher than that. In fact when I came up with this quiz, I thought the answer was 16, only to realise I had been duped by my own test.

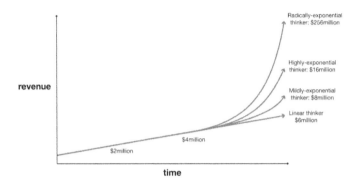

This is something we can see over and over again. This is why Einstein called compounding effects the 8th Wonder of the World. Here are a few more examples to illustrate this.

The Law of Accelerating Returns & the Human Genome Project

We won't experience 100 years of progress in the 21st century — it will be more like 20,000 years of progress.
- Ray Kurzweil

We couldn't talk about the idea of exponential growth and therefore exponential thinking without mentioning Moore's

Law and Ray Kurzweil. In 1965, Gordon Moore, a co-founder of the company which later became Intel, was asked to predict the next ten years of the semiconductor (computer microchips) industry. Based on his observations, Moore anticipated that the number of transistors in a dense integrated circuit, hence the power of computers, would double approximately every two years for the next ten years. This became known as Moore's Law, a symbol of the exponential rate of technological progression.

In 2001, futurist Ray Kurzweil extended Gordon Moore's predictions further. In his seminal essay *'The Law of Accelerating Returns'* he puts an eloquent finger on this notion that people tend to assume the rate of change will continue at its current pace. The fallacy in this, is that when we zoom in on any given period of an exponential curve, it looks flat. Just as the Earth looks and feels flat from our tiny, zoomed-in human perspective. But if we take a metaphorical rocket up into space, and reach a zoomed-out perspective, we can see the curve. And often this curve is exponential, getting steeper and steeper like a hockey stick. Kurzweil even goes further as to say that:

> *One can examine the data in different ways, on different time scales, and for a wide variety of technologies ranging from electronic to biological,*

and the acceleration of progress and growth
applies. Indeed, we find not just simple exponential
growth, but 'double' exponential growth, meaning
that the rate of exponential growth is itself growing
exponentially.

He explains this through the application of positive feedback loops, a key concept of systems thinking which we've touched on already.

I digress into theory behind all this, but I think it's important to touch on these fundamental principles as they give us context for the world that we live in and for why our reaction to this world is being far outpaced by the pace of change itself. This difficulty to compute exponentially could be putting our civilisation and our planet in danger. Kurzweil has a very good illustration of this gap between what he calls *"the Intuitive Linear View"* versus *"the Historical Exponential View"*. He says:

> *When the human genome project started fourteen*
> *years ago, critics pointed out that given the speed*
> *with which the genome could then be scanned, it*
> *would take thousands of years to finish the project.*
> *Yet the fifteen year project was nonetheless*
> *completed slightly ahead of schedule.*

A clear example of this gulf between reality and how we predict it.

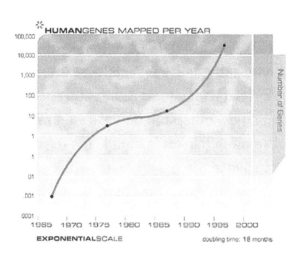

- From Ray Kurzweil's 2001 essay *'The Law of Accelerating Returns'*

If you'd like to test this gap in perception at home, I suggest you have a conversation about the future with somebody from an older generation. Recently, I spoke to my godfather about driverless cars. Putting aside the debate we had over whether they were better drivers than humans or whether it was ethically okay to allow computers to make decisions that could result in the injury or death of humans, we discussed how long it would take to happen. On the basis he'd never actually seen one before, although had heard plenty on the news, my godfather wasn't even sure it would happen at all, if it did he said this wouldn't be for a very very long time which I interpreted as 'not in my lifetime'. A couple of months later, in August 2016, Uber tested driverless taxis for the first time in the USA. Now this is very far from mass adoption but it is a good illustration of how we struggle to see how steep the curve is when we're too close to it. We often think this stuff is the future, but to think that is to live in the past, because these ideas are here today in the present. This I think is the mistake made by so many CEOs and their (in retrospect) amusing quotes denying the potentially disruptive power of a new competitor. Here are a few fun ones:

Steve Ballmer, former CEO of Microsoft on Apple's iPhone in 2007
There's no chance that the iPhone is going to get any significant market share. No chance. It's a $500 subsidized item. They may make a lot of money. But if you actually take a look at the 1.3 billion phones that get sold, I'd prefer to have our software in 60% or 70% or 80% of them, than I would to have 2% or 3%, which is what Apple might get.
- Steve Ballmer, 2007

Marriott CEO Arne Sorenson on Airbnb in 2014
Sorenson originally dismissed Airbnb as an *"interesting experiment"* that was *"fun to watch."* Later on, when Airbnb CEO Brian Chesky learned that Marriott International planned to add 30,000 rooms to its property portfolio in the coming year, he defiantly boasted, *"We will add that to our portfolio in the next 2 weeks."*

Thomas Watson, president of IBM, in 1943
"I think there is a world market for maybe five computers."

This one is perhaps a little mean, and it's important to say that all of these people are super smart, and they're working largely within their own paradigm and information bubble. What is important to take away is the sheer scale and speed of the transformations. Thomas Watson was literally the best placed person in 1943 to predict the growth of computers, and he got it monumentally wrong. Just imagine what we're getting wrong right now?

The limits of centralisation and the obvious exponential effect of a distributed system

So we've established through these examples and through the predictions of some very clever people that we tend to assume linear progression in an exponentially progressing world. The Airbnb example though I think gives us an interesting argument to suggest that centralised organisations (in this case Marriott) are not operating on exponential models because they are constrained by the limitations of centralisation. If we react in a centralised way, the speed of our reaction will be linear due to the numerical constraints created by the bottleneck of hierarchy and centralisation. The potential for growth of a decentralised system which doesn't operate according to a hierarchy is numerically far superior due to its ability to activate dormant nodes in the wider system, recycling waste (in this case the nodes are existing empty houses). Not only is this numerically superior, but the many nodes in a distributed network are able to operate simultaneously. Thus, a decentralised organisation has the potential to widen that gap between dormancy and activity at a rapid rate, with a speed exponentially surpassing the speed at which a centralised hierarchical organisation can react. Sadly this also could be the case for our planet. Our highly centralised governments are reacting in a linear fashion to a time bomb where the seconds are ticking faster and faster and getting shorter and shorter.

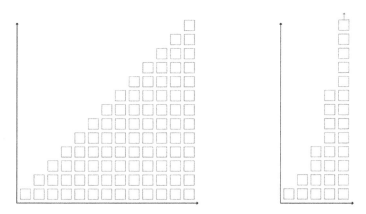

Centralised system

Illustration of a centralised system, with linear year on year growth. For instance, if it were to add new hotels every year.
Equation: 1 + 1 + 1 + 1 ...

Networked system

Illustration of a networked system, exponential year on year growth. For instance, if it were to make use of existing empty houses in the network.
Equation: 1 x 2 x 2 x 2 x ...

I've come to the belief that it is mathematically impossible to deal with so much complexity through a centralised system. If I go to the ends of my beliefs here, I think that operating within the traditional limits of centralised governments, banks, hospitals...etc is limiting to human cultural evolution, and is preventing us from moving forward as a species. Luckily, I also think that the genie's been let out of the bottle and there's no putting it back in. A world where 7 billion people live online isn't just a prediction, it's an inevitability. In that world, the internet becomes the fundamental element in a human operating system which inherently protects our intent to evolve.

Applying the exponentiality of networks back to democracy

The networked economy as exhibited by the exponential growth of organisations such as Uber, Airbnb, and Apple could serve as an indicator of the potential for a digitally distributed direct democracy. A system which activates the nodes that are currently dormant in a hierarchical and centralised structure where information goes up and down a narrow ladder. The pipes are far bigger in a distributed system, or at least there are way more pipes for the information to flow through. Our bandwidth is greater and therefore the number of inputs and the speed at which we give those inputs is far higher. In this kind of system our ability to change society could finally catch up with the speed at which the world is actually moving.

In the current linear structure, the slowness of our reactions is creating a greater and greater gap with the exponential reality that we live in. Our solution to this must surely be to recycle the wasted potential of our networked system and engage in deeper dialogue with self-organised communities. We will be evolving humanity exponentially, just as these globally distributed business models do. It comes down to simple maths. How many decisions can one centralised government make in a year versus an entire population, or even a fractal subset of communities deciding on issues directly concerning them? The number of decisions needed is far surpassing the speed of decision-making that our centralised governments operate at. The pipes are full and our 'democratic internet' is at a standstill. Moving to a peer-to-peer direct democracy may allow us to get back on track and upgrade to a much faster operating system for humanity, to evolve to our next stage.

Unlearning our assumptions about 'how democracy works'

This is a new world and the biggest shift I think we need to make is in the assumptions we hold as to 'how the world is'. These static beliefs are informing adverse behaviours which stifle our natural evolution. Therefore when reading the stories, models, theories and hypotheses in this book, I'd like to ask you to try and dispel the following assumptions in your mind. You may choose to still hold these beliefs when you've read the whole thing, but until then, please try to ignore the devil on your shoulder. In the famous words of renowned futurist Alvin Toffler:

> *The illiterate of the 21st century will not be those who cannot read or write, but those who cannot learn, unlearn, and relearn.*

So, here are 15 assumptions to put aside for this book:

1. Democracy means voting for one option or another
2. Central governance is essential to running a country
3. We need representatives and we vote for people
4. Politics requires politicians and parties
5. We vote on a cyclical basis (e.g. every 4 years)
6. Voting is our only voice
7. We belong to a country
8. Countries are only geographically defined
9. Companies, countries, NGOs are different things
10. We rely on governments to provide our public services
11. We need small groups to decide for us, not everybody

can participate and create good work

12. 'Experts' are right
13. There is such a thing as an 'expert'
14. Large groups can't make good decisions
15. The system we have now won't change for a long time

If you can suspend these 15 assumptions for a while, then we should end this story with a new vision of what I believe is an undeniably different and unprecedented shift in the way the world works. The democratic system could be about to get some rocket fuel up its arse.

A computer is the most remarkable tool that we have ever come up with. It's a bicycle for our minds.

- Steve Jobs

part 2: inspiration. where might we be going?

Now we've explored the rapid impact that tech is having on our lives, and we have some context for this mad mad world that we find ourselves in. Let's look in detail at some examples from other fields to see this change in action through a microcosmic lens. By putting these examples together we will move towards a sketch of what the bigger picture could look like. A picture that provides the background for our revolutionary tech democracy protagonists from around the world.

Inspiration from the world of work

The ability technology has to distribute power is remarkable, and if the world of work is anything to go by, there are some hopeful signs that this distribution is becoming ever more deeply embedded in the modern psyche. What we can see as a result of this is a breed of highly evolved organisations operating on decentralised principles.

This is nothing new of course. It was almost 10 years ago

that I first got hooked on thinking about changing the world of work and I had the idea of founding my organisational re-design studio, **flux**. I probably first considered writing this book when I read the story of a now famous Brazilian company, Semco. An unusual company run by an inspiring and wise man called Ricardo Semler. In 1980, Ricardo Semler inherited his father's company. It wasn't doing particularly well, so his solution to this was an approach which has since been referred to as 'participative management' or 'democratic management'. He basically decided to put the people in charge: truly in charge. He made all of the financial information open, gave people flexibility over where and when they worked, allowed people to set their own salaries, gave freedom for workers to setup their own ventures, and gradually implemented a host of other such initiatives. Basically he treated them like adults. Radical, I know. What is remarkable to me is that he had the instinct to use these innovative methods before the internet really showed us what it could do. How it could connect people, start movements, allow people to organise...etc. To me it's like he was operating ahead of his time, before the soil was fertile to plant these ideas.

Distributed organisations

This story which Semler documents beautifully in his

books *'Maverick'* and *'The Seven Day Weekend'* were a revelation to me, and it seems many others. In 2014, Frederic Laloux wrote a book called *'Reinventing Organisations'* which has sparked a reasonable community around it. Laloux's basic premise is that for every stage of human evolution, humans have created new methods of organising ourselves. From the military organisations, to big industry, to companies that value their culture and people almost like family, to what he calls *"Evolutionary Organisations"*. These are at the pinnacle of Laloux's evolutionary hierarchy. And there are examples of these organisations spread across the world, from very diverse industries, which, without consulting or even having any prior knowledge of each other, seem to have developed a similar set of practices. Laloux posits that these practices are underpinned by three core principles: purposeful, authentic, and self-managed. Perhaps the most poignant element I take from Frederic's work though is:

> *The age of the internet has precipitated a new worldview - one that can contemplate the possibility of distributed intelligence instead of top-down hierarchy.*
> - Frederic Laloux, Reinventing Organisations

This is something that also came up in a specific part of

my conversation with Colin Megill, a co-founder of pol.is who you will hear more from later on. He said:

Organizations are finding that a lot of the wisdom is at the nodes of the organization, the edges of the organization rather than in the center. The organizations who are taking advantage of that, like Tesla for instance, are moving very quickly. As the world accelerates, organizational technology is going to be able to move decision making into the outside of the organization. And they're going to move faster, and operate with more information.

This notion of a distributed organisation is very clear in the various stories that exemplify this movement and philosophy. There are stories of companies like Buurtzorg, the Dutch neighborhood nursing company, where the CEO has no more say in the direction of the company that the employees. His role is to coach them and 'hold' the vision. The 9,000-person strong company is comprised of teams of 12 self-managed nurses who make the decisions they think are best for their patients. No asking for permission from central office or waiting for the idea to be approved, or for there to be a consistent standard across all teams. They do what they think is best because they are so close to the customer. In fact, out of the 9,000 team members at Buurtzorg, only about 40 work in a central office, and they have no more power than any of the nurses, their role is to support them in doing the best job they can. It resembles what Netflix have termed *"a culture of freedom and responsibility"*. They have the freedom to make their own decisions and do what they think is right, and equally they are responsible for the outcome.

In the networked age, we hear no shortage of new modes of organisation or curious cultures that really focus on giving people control over their lives. From Google, to Facebook, to Zappos, Silicon Valley and the tech world at large has totally pioneered a next generation of management and organisational methodologies born out of the necessity presented by the speed of change and the complexity of creating value in an environment of extreme uncertainty. I think this is why the field of organisational development is perhaps a natural place to look when we're examining innovative ways of organising ourselves at a larger scale: at a social, political and governmental level. For-profit organisations need to constantly evolve to compete in a Darwinian environment, they have many stakeholders, they have to innovate and try new things to survive, and they have to move very quickly in a world where technology is developing at an exponential pace. This has resulted in many different management doctrines and organisational models, but the most succinct and broadly indicative one that I have come across is the 'ResponsiveOrg Manifesto' written by Aaron Dignan, Adam Pisoni, Matthew Partovi, Mike Arauz and Steve Hopkins. This is a movement and community of practitioners looking to transform theirs and their clients' organisations in a world which is less and less predictable. The manifesto is most simply explained with 5 binary scales:

The challenges we face are becoming less and less predictable. Those practices that were so successful in the past are counter-productive in less predictable environments. In contrast, Responsive Organizations are designed to thrive in less predictable environments by balancing the following tensions:

Profit <-> Purpose
Hierarchies <-> Networks
Controlling <-> Empowering
Planning <-> Experimentation
Privacy <-> Transparency

- from Responsive.org

As I mentioned before, the notions that underpin the shifts in organisational practices seem to be based on a few factors: speed, complexity and creativity. Speed to move quickly but also to adapt to the external world moving quickly. Complexity because there is no single way of doing things anymore. Creativity because moving quickly in an unknown environment requires novel solutions. To me, if this is relevant on an organisational level, it is only exaggerated and increasingly necessary on a macro level. I see these organisational models as pointers towards what might be possible on a global or national level (if that is indeed something that still exists in the future) if we use technology to get the scale needed, to access the collective intelligence needed, and to work at the speed required to *"minimise existential threat to humanity"* as Elon Musk so succinctly puts it in his description of the philosophy which powers SolarCity, Tesla and SpaceX.

Lessons from agile & lean manufacturing

The best known and probably most fundamental breakthroughs in organisational methodology are the lean and agile movements. These approaches to organisation and value creation are for the most part sorely lacking in the way our governments and nations are run, yet they have a valuable alternative perspective on risk and a 'maker's' approach to developing the future.

The origins of lean principles are to be found in the Toyota car manufacturing plant, and were developed in the mid-20th century. The most interesting element of which (for our purposes) is the concept of 'Kaizen', Japanese for *"improvement"*. And in a business context, this means a continual improvement. The kind that cuts across all levels of a hierarchy and all business units. It is a mindset as much as it is a strict working process. Kaizen means that everything is up for grabs. Everything is editable. Everything can be improved, incrementally, little by little, forever. Kaizen never stops. There's no ultimate goal here, other than continual improvement.

On Toyota production lines, right up until 2014, there was something called the Andon cord that hung above the workers heads, well within reach. If anything at all went wrong on the line, the workers would pull the cord and the line would stop with a pleasant chime. They would all work as long as it took fix the problem, without rushing, then log the incident and restart the line. The logic here was to reduce waste by making sure that everything came off the line as intended. There was no waste. Everyone had the authority to pull the cord, everyone contributed solutions to problems, and they did so for the greater good of the production process.

Lean principles have combined with Agile principles in modern evolved organisations to create fast-moving, constantly updating systems for value creation.

Agile emerged in 2001 as a set of simple principles for advanced software development practices. The group who built the initiative wanted to move away from an old 'waterfall' way of doing things, where long-term planning and elaborate Gantt-chart-style project management techniques defined their workflow; towards agile and responsive methods where constant iteration, rapid release cycles, and self-managing teams defined their process. The movement focused around four statements:

> ***Individuals and interactions*** *over processes and tools*
> ***Working software*** *over comprehensive documentation*
> ***Customer collaboration*** *over contract negotiation*
> ***Responding to change*** *over following a plan*

Over the last 15 years the principles of Agile have expanded far beyond the world of software development to design agencies, startups, innovation labs, and companies all over the world. The core philosophy remains but its implementation is radically different depending on the organisation and industry.

Both Agile and Lean put full emphasis on the creation of

value way beyond the creation of documentation. In a world where bureaucracy is a pretty common pain point for people, this is a principle that I'm sure many would love to see in the way society is run. In addition to that, these movements put huge focus on involving the customer in the creation of the product. Through constant feedback loops, the team creating the product are able to gain a deeper understanding of what their customers and users need and to ensure their product is having the impact they want it to have. Compare this to the system of infrequent referenda (plebiscites), general elections, or petitions and we can easily see how we could transfer learnings across from the kind of work pioneered by manufacturing and software companies. In fact it's pretty common for political parties to create their manifestos without even asking the people what they think. How is it even possible to enact the will of the people if you don't know what the people actually want?! This is because the dualistic, combative party system is based on outdated and frozen ideologies. More about that later though, I'll let somebody far smarter and more pragmatic than me rant about that one. Back to the world of work.

Another important element to these evolved working practices is the ambition for 'all work to be visible'. Any time anybody does anything, everybody should be able to see it. The possibilities for learning are therefore far more frequent, much faster, and readily accessible. This is part of the reason why many startups move and scale so quickly. Comparing this to countries or other such entities, there are many amazing things happening in small pockets but these lessons are often not shared for the whole system to benefit from. A good analogy for this is to think about how many driverless car networks function. The advantage of multiple cars being connected together over a wireless network is that when one car makes a mistake, all cars benefit from the lesson that comes out of that event: paving the way for exponential learning.

This notion of iteration and improvement is at the core of these distributed methods of working. Making the most of the network, we are able to test and improve constantly in different areas simultaneously, learning from each other. This is partly why companies have 'accelerators' and 'incubators', so that they can constantly learn and grow at speed. Seeing this transferred to a macro level could lead to us testing a new way of fighting drugs in one place, whilst testing a new approach to education in another, and a new punitive system in another. The lessons are shared around and the whole system grows. What works is replicated elsewhere, what doesn't work never spreads far enough to cause significant harm. The notion of risk is totally reversed because of the decentralised nature of such a system. There is massive risk in not trying things very quickly in small pockets. Some countries already work like this to a limited extent. Think about the minimally devolved powers of US states, Swiss cantons, or UK countries. But what we're suggested here is radical devolution of power to support experimentation and accelerate cultural evolution.

Citizen centricity

There is a school of thinking in the world of innovation which says, companies that are winning their various races are those that are most focused on solving their customers 'human needs', on truly understanding people and creating products and services which really fulfil them. This philosophy is visible in practices like Design Thinking and Jobs To Be Done, the creator of the latter, Clayton Christensen asserts that *"customers don't buy brands or products. They hire solutions to get jobs done."* This has led to companies like Zappos putting astonishing emphasis on giving employees all the power they need for solving their customers' problems. It has also led to a real shift from focusing on the technology we produce, to designing experiences which fulfill the needs of the people our products serve. It's no surprise that Flickr, Kickstarter, Airbnb, Slack, Pinterest and Tumblr were all founded by designers, who are trained to solve problems for people through design.

What does this mean for democracy? I don't know what our governments as entities will look like when we eventually revolutionise our social operating system, but I'm convinced that if there is such an entity as a government, they will have to be far closer to the customer, or in our case, the citizen. This may mean putting citizens in control, and shortening the distance between two ends of the value chain: something analogous to what Soundcloud does by removing all of the music industry's middle men, and shortening the distance between a musician and an audience. Or it may mean a government looks more like customer service from a company. One that really empowers team members to do what is necessary to fulfil our human needs. Either way, the clutter and waste in between the person and policy will have to be removed. Waste is slowing us down from creating frequent, direct and meaningful change in our communities. We will explore a pretty radical example of how this can work with our Estonian e-Residency friend Kaspar later, who is using citizen feedback to change real legislation much faster than a government would traditionally be able to.

Returning to our human-need-focused business practices, the first stage of the Design Thinking process tends to be an 'empathic' stage where customers are interviewed in-depth for the designers to truly understand their needs. At a governmental level, there is rarely a forum for this to happen, at least not on a deep level. This sounds absurd when we think about how a tech company would never even consider making products or services without asking customers what they really need on a fundamental human level. To not do so is to assume that we know what everybody in our countries thinks and feels. No wonder some heads of state develop dangerous senses of entitlement.

We need systems which are built to just listen to citizens, to interview them, to understand what we need. To then turn these needs into opportunities for services and solutions that advance society. Design is a key ingredient to the creation of a better environment for us all to live in. Some efforts have been made, in the UK for instance with the creation of the Government Digital Service (GDS) who are working on the British Government's digital transformation using Design Thinking, Lean, and Agile methodologies. In their words:

> *"We always start with user needs. We are agile. We work to a set of Design Principles that guide us in everything we do."*

These are the principles they have outlined for the current and future development of UK digital services:

1. Start with needs (user needs not government needs)
2. Do less
3. Design with data
4. Do the hard work to make it simple
5. Iterate. Then iterate again.
6. This is for everyone (thanks again Tim!)
7. Understand context
8. Build digital services, not websites
9. Be consistent, not uniform
10. Make things open: it makes things better

These principles are pretty indistinguishable from those of almost any best-in-practice tech giant or startup. GDS has a vision to transform the way we think about government, from a bloated, arcane monster to a digital platform.

"Siloed approaches to transformation don't work. Reinventing the wheel every single time we build a service has led to far too much duplication and waste. That's not good enough.

We want to fix that by building Government as a

Platform.

*Government as a Platform is a new vision for digital
government; a common core infrastructure of
shared digital systems, technology and processes
on which it's easy to build brilliant, user-centric
government services."*
- from the Government Digital Service Blog

The term 'Government as a Platform' was coined by the
tech and internet legend Tim O'Reilly. In an article for
Forbes in 2009 he laid out his vision for the future of a
"tech-powered government".

*How does government itself become an open
platform that allows people inside and outside
government to innovate? How do you design a
system in which all of the outcomes aren't specified
beforehand, but instead evolve through interactions
between the technology provider and its user
community?*

*This is a radical departure from the old model of
government, which Donald Kettl so aptly named
'vending machine government.' We pay our taxes;
we get back services. And when we don't get what
we expect, our 'participation' is limited to protest–*

essentially, shaking the vending machine.
- Tim O'Reilly, *Gov 2.0: The Promise Of Innovation*
in Forbes

Powerful visionary stuff from a pioneering mind. And as you might imagine, I couldn't agree more.

From powerful people to powerful processes

To those readers who perhaps don't work in the world of software, startups or other industries which have been quick at adopting evolved ways of organising their businesses, this might all seem like chaos. The key however to these methods is not that we take out hierarchy, or bureaucracy and replace it with nothing at all, creating a big vacuum, it is simply that we shift power from 'people' to 'processes'. So, if anything, there is more process, or at least the process are valued and questioned all the time, and are constantly improving the product. This is known as a 'dynamic system'. John Buck, an expert on Sociocracy puts it this way:

> *In physics, an element that is changing is referred to as dynamic. Thus, a dynamic environment is one that is unstable, or capable of change, as opposed to being static, or incapable of change. Since our*

natural environment is dynamic, our most effective organisations will be those that are dynamic as well, those that can change in response to both internal and external changes, whether they are pressures or opportunities, adapting in much the same way a living organism adapts.

The 'Sociocratic' method of management was developed in its current form in 1970s by Dutch entrepreneur Gerard Endenburg. There are many specificities to this model which I won't go into here (you can read John Buck's book, *'We the People'*) but the key thing that I'd like to draw attention to is the shift from powerful people to powerful processes as well as the notion of constant change.

Rather than operating according to static departments or layers of hierarchical decision-making and communication flows, Sociocracy works with 'circles'. Each circle works towards a clearly defined vision with specific roles, aims and processes that provide the circle with what they need to meet their goals, as well as sharing their lessons with other groups.

Deciding how we decide

In the absence of formal autocracy, an interesting element

to Sociocracy is that circles have 'operational meetings' where they focus on what they're working on, and 'policy meetings' where they focus on how they're working. For those of you more familiar with Holacracy, a modern twist on Sociocracy, these have been branded by HolacracyOne as 'tactical meetings' and 'governance meetings'. I simply call them 'what meetings' and 'how meetings'. So whilst most people in more traditional organisation put a lot of emphasis on meeting to answer 'What?' Here there is equal importance placed on answering 'How?'

The result of this is a process of constant tweaks to the underlying fabric of how an organisation is organised. This means that roles change, teams change, guidelines change...etc. And a beautiful consequence of this is that the shape of the organisation as a whole is always changing. The idea is to move away from infrequent, expensive, large-scale organisational redesign overhauls every decade or so, and instead create a system that constantly adapts. Essentially, they are constantly updating their operating system like your phone does with its apps, releasing the latest bug fixes to the way they 'decide how they decide'. To do that on a macro-level could perhaps be the greatest win of them all.

In an email exchange, John Buck explained one of the

underpinning reasons why models like Sociocracy could point towards forms of governance which can work in the internet age:

> We can see how fractals arise out of circular equations. By analogy, soon as you introduce circular power (a la Sociocracy and Agile) you move from complicated to complex. The internet increases feedback (circularity) so much that it makes the world much more complex. Therefore, we must have circular governance systems to match the complexity. Life is a complex system because it is capable of repairing itself (circularity). When we make governance complex, it becomes a living form. A series of fractals, or circles inside circles inside circles.

Uh, what do you mean by a 'fractal' John?! Wikipedia says:

> A fractal is a curve or geometric figure, each part of which has the same statistical character as the whole. They are useful in modelling structures (such as snowflakes) in which similar patterns recur at progressively smaller scales, and in describing partly random or chaotic phenomena such as crystal growth and galaxy formation.

Here's a couple of fractal visualisations which may help. For the sake of basic understanding, see them as charts of how people could organise themselves:

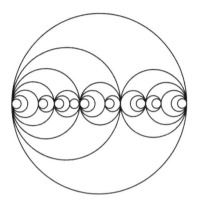

There is a good diagram by Tony Hsieh, the CEO of Zappos which shows this phenomenon as they adopt Sociocratic methods (Holacracy specifically). I've made a stripped back version here:

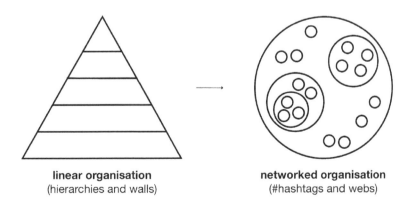

linear organisation
(hierarchies and walls)

networked organisation
(#hashtags and webs)

Sociocracy is perhaps the most clearly structured model we have today for organisations to function like 'living systems' which evolve, learn, grow and gain from disorder. It is in the early stages of its maturation as a social technology, but its underpinning notion of circularity or fractals is a huge and important mindset shift for the way we see the world and organise our governments. A vision of fractals with constant feedback loops could point towards a model which is genuinely scalable to a societal and governmental level.

The beauty of the vision is that with each fractal operating as a self-managed cell, they are able to work with the real needs of the people who form that cell: a citizen-centric cell in the case of a new democratic system. Each cell could then be linked to one another with communication-based lead roles which technology could easily facilitate at a larger scale. The linking of these cells allows for each element of the fractal to operate with inertia whilst also giving feedback and receiving feedback from each other cell at each level of society.

Bear with me here, but John Buck has a great analogy he borrows from research he has done in nature. The organic system he uses to describe great feedback systems is the octopus. He broke this down for me with the following characteristics of an octopus:

- Each leg has a personality

- Each leg can feed-forward & feed-back with its external environment

- It coordinates these eight different world views

- It has a true collective mind

- Only 10% of the entire nervous system is in the central brain

Replace each leg with a sub-fractal or cell in an country or state and interconnect them. There we have a great metaphor for how humans could organise ourselves.

The weird thing is that society is actually kind of working like this already. Each part is affecting each part, we just don't see the causalities and correlations because of the complexities and speed of the modern world. The mind-made structures we have created to simplify complexity only simplify the complications in our minds but have no effect on complexity itself. In organisations, departments don't actually exist, org charts don't actually exist, these are all artificial articulations of the world we wish we lived in. Adopting fractals as a metaphor for governance gives us a lens through which to see the interconnectedness of everything in the world without reducing it to over-simplistic charts and diagrams.

Beyond winners and losers: the implied divisiveness of democracy

Now, the title of this book is 'democracy' squared, but is democracy even the right thing to be talking about here? First of all, what is it? I think the term democracy is maybe at its purest defined as 'government of the people by the people', however:

> In modern times it has become equated to elections or "a system of government in which all the people of a state or polity....elect representatives to a parliament or similar assembly."
> - Oxford English Dictionary & Wikipedia

The *"in modern times"* bit I think is quite significant here. I'm not sure this notion of elected representatives is actually at the core of democracy, I think it's probably what mass pseudo-participation looked like in an analogue world. The previous sections on technology show that this may not be necessary, and the case study projects coming up in the next chapter pretty much confirm that. But is it worth democratising democracy if it's the wrong system to operate from in the first place? Let's examine democracy as a decision making system rather than a social structure to understand this a little more. Here's a brief and simplified articulation of the different forms that governance has typically taken, as inspired by John Buck:

Autocratic decision making
One person or entity tells others how things are.
Pros: Can be quick up to a certain capacity, can have clear direction if the autocratic is somehow enlightened
Cons: It is highly highly improbable that one source has the answers to all problems. Particularly wicked problems which are intertwined in systemic complexity. It's pretty horrible to be a part of for most people, except for the autocrat and the demographic that he (autocrats are almost always a 'he') is affiliated with.

Democratic decision making
We can all vote on whether we're 'in' or 'out', 'yes' or 'no', 'republican' or 'democrat', 'blues or reds'
Pros: We all get to feel involved, multiple perspectives are considered. We (kind of) avoid being ruled by corrupt tyrants.
Cons: By definition this creates a majority and minority where the majority now rules the minority. And with great power comes great responsibility so in that system there

is the majority must basically look after the minority, something we historically haven't done so well as a species. Democracy is therefore divisive by nature.

Consensus decision making
We all agree on the decision.
Pros: We all agree on the decision. We get different in-depth perspectives. We are all engaged.
Cons: It can be exhausting. It can take ages or even totally halt. It can drastically water down ideas and proposals. Remember the old joke: *"the camel was a horse designed by consensus"*.

Consent based decision making
We can input and feedback but the proposal still goes ahead unless anybody has any 'paramount objections' (a paramount objection being a decision that is 'outside of the person's range of tolerance', i.e. they couldn't cope with this decision)
Pros: We can move quickly even as a group. We can still input. We can test things. There is still a safety measure in place.
Cons: When poorly implemented can result in 'veto-like' behaviour. This is avoidable if adapted though as we'll see with some practical examples.

It's clear that evolved organisations tend to use more

consent based decision making processes than the other three. That's the one we should be aiming for in our new democratic structures. And the single transferable vote is one way that we might enact that. Whilst traditionally voting systems are binary or simplistic (In or Out, Left or Right, one person one vote) this can also be adapted as with the single transferable voting system which is used in some places at various levels of government (Ireland, Malta, Australia). Here you get to rank the different options, be they candidates or policies, with a league table being formed in the end. This enables the decision to be less binary and more representative of the overall population's beliefs. There is more granularity to this system basically. Another pro of this system is that it can avoid a situation in binary voting terms where a lot of people submit a protest vote, sometimes known as the 'fuck you vote'. This was pretty obvious during the British referendum on the EU. With the single transferable voting system, this discontent with the existing system can still be expressed whilst not clouding the overall complex decision held by the general population. This system basically allows for nuance. We see this system used in progressive systems we'll be exploring like MiVote in Australia or with part of the Icelandic Crowdsourced Constitution's process. A combination of a sort of mass consent-based decision making, whilst sticking to more traditional voting methods.

The democratic value chain

We've looked at the methods and systems that different types of organisations are using to work at a rapid pace in harmony with complexity. Now I'd like to discuss the business models and particularly the typical value chain that has evolved in the internet-age, to the often catastrophic detriment of many companies. There are many examples of this in publishing, travel, marketing, and film, but the best example I can think of is the music industry.

The way the value chain in the record industry (note the word 'record') used to look something like this:

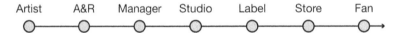

Traditional record industry value chain, pre-internet
Many stakeholders, artist & fan far removed

New entertainment industry value chain, post-internet
Few stakeholders, artist & fan are close

This business model essentially cuts out the middleman, or at least combines the middlemen. HMV and Blockbusters were swiftly replaced by Spotify and Netflix. The impact of these new models is often referred to as the 'democratising' of an industry. Currently our political decision making process is far from democratised. Or at least the democratic supply chain is very far from lean. Of course it depends on the country or district, but a common supply chain for indirect democracy looks something like this:

Traditional democratic value chain, pre internet
Many stakeholders, policies & citizens far removed

If democratising democracy is to follow the same pattern as the countless industries which have been disrupted, what would that look like?

New democratic value chain, post-internet
Few stakeholders, policy & citizen are close

These convoluted supply chains were necessary pre-technology and pre-networked society. Everything was somehow further away from everything else, and we didn't have the tech infrastructure for mass participation. This just isn't the case anymore. There is no technical barrier whatsoever to a whole nation deciding on policies directly rather than going through various layers of government, and moving along the value chain. It would be faster, involve more people...etc.

The way I see it, representative democracy is largely underpinned by a couple of outdated assumptions. First is that before the internet it wasn't possible to involve everybody. Nothing would ever get done. So the only way to do democracy was to pass on your vote to somebody you trust, somebody who would represent you. That made sense back then, but now we *do* have the internet. This argument for passing on my vote on how the world runs makes little sense from a functional perspective.

The second is that some people think other people aren't smart enough to really have a say, so representative democracy is a way of giving those people a fake say in the way the world runs. Yet when we pit expert traders versus random crowds we often see that the so-called experts tend to do worse in predicting market fluctuations.

The modern world is far far too complex to think that a group of old middle class people (probably men) in a room could possibly have all the knowledge they need to make good decisions all the time without asking the wider public. Again, now we have the technology to access experts in any field, and mix that with the crowd's view of the world.

So the role of representatives as it stands doesn't really make sense in the internet age as far as I can see. This isn't to say some form of public representative won't be needed in the future, simply that the function that role will serve needs to change, along with the skillsets and attitudes of the people.

So what about presidents and prime ministers? I obviously don't know what will *actually* happen, but it isn't inconceivable to think those roles could rapidly become redundant if we democratise democracy. In the end, in a new system it will be for the people to decide how we decide. But the amateur futurist in me is willing to bet that these official roles will be superseded by meritocratic or visionary social leaders. The movements led by these individuals will live and die by whether they demonstrate legitimacy. Think of the many social movements in history, from Harvey Milk, to Mahatma Gandhi, to Simone De Beauvoir, to Rosa Luxemburg, to Toussaint

L'Ouverture, to Emiliano Zapata, to Leon Trotsky, to Aung San Suu Kyi, to Che Guevara, to Nelson Mandela: the world has been full of legitimate non-formal leaders who made a massive dent in the universe. None of whom held official office during their most radical periods of leading change.

If democracy is democratised, these visionary leaders could move from being underground movements culminating in protests, to becoming a wide range of different sets of communal beliefs validated by legitimate power. Because, although the media fanfare behind representative elections in some countries may seem like ebullient sporting commentary. It isn't. Thinking of our social decisions as simply as Blue vs Red is ridiculous in a complex world. Technology may be built on binary but it is allowing operating systems which are far more nuanced than the dualistic notions of party lines being towed. Distributed democracy will finally allow the people's line to be towed. And for multiple social movements to evolve and flourish in a genuinely diversified democracy.

Obviously there is one little problem though…

Learning from history

If we are to learn from history however, this may not be so

easy to achieve. The record industry remains our perfect comparison point for this. When Napster turned up with P2P technology which cut out all the middlemen, the record labels' immediate reaction was to sue Napster in a pathetic attempt to fight the inevitable evolutionary shift society was undergoing. It took iTunes and later Spotify to turn up and make use of technology to offer a genuine alternative to both the traditional model and to free downloading. The *suits* were literally fighting the *pirates* in the case of the P2P torrent-based repository, Pirate Bay.

So what does this mean for politics? Well, I don't think I'd be causing too much offence in leaning on the stereotype that some politicians may have personal agendas. When technology is finally used to cut them out of the value chain, what will their reaction be? It will take our most progressive leaders to actively leave space and use technology to democratise democracy. Old roles will become extinct and make room for new and different roles which we'll explore in the next part, particularly in the example of the Icelandic *Crowdsourced Constitution*.

Anti-fragility: reframing our approach to risk

Above I briefly mentioned risk and how we might need to look at it differently. Our difficulty in changing our beliefs around risk are very similar to the difficulties we discussed in reframing our approach to strongly held beliefs such as trust. A common expression in Silicon Valley, and amongst tech startups in general, is the expression *"fail fast"*. An easy articulation of the relationship that exponential organisations have with risk.

To stereotype, whilst big organisations often have long reports, extensive strategic analyses, and spend months crafting business cases, lean organisations advance through trial and error. Part of the logic being that where traditionally you might research something for 18 months, at the end of which you either find that it doesn't work or that somebody else has launched the same thing in the interim. But it's far cheaper and faster and smarter to simply build and test a low-fi version to learn immediately whether it's worth building on or giving up. This notion of risk is I think a concept that we need to rewire in our brains, particularly in schools if we are to adapt and create in the world of today. It is more costly to not try things. This isn't a throwaway comment. It is pretty much a fact.

This partly explains the iterative & distributed organisations we looked at in the previous chapter which are sometimes described as 'anti-fragile organisations' referencing Nassim Taleb's awesome book, *Anti-Fragile:*

Things That Gain From Disorder. These organisations' approach to risk is one whereby they know that they can grow from *"negative events"*. To quote Frederik Nietzsche: *"What doesn't kills us makes us stronger."*

Now, I am no way smart enough to summarise this highly intellectual and robust work, so at the risk of bastardising it, I'm going to give it a go anyway.

Anti-fragility is essentially a term used to define anything which improves when it undergoes stress. The most well known example of an anti-fragile act is probably the vaccine. As we know, vaccines work by injecting a small stressor into the body. The immune system then reacts by learning to combat this stressor. The dosage of that stressor is the key. The body isn't able to withstand a full-blown illness, but a small quantity of that illness can help it get stronger. The expression *wrapping your kids in cotton wool*, not letting them experience danger or risk at any level, is the antithesis of this, and is a very fragile behaviour.

So we've seen above that humans tend to think of things as static, and to think about development in a linear way. In everyday logic, we define a glass as fragile because it breaks when it falls, and a rock as robust because it doesn't. Something anti-fragile actually gets stronger when it falls, i.e. when it undergoes small shots of stress. This is very simplified analogous explanation of the term of course.

Now if we think of systems as a whole it becomes easier to see how a system can be anti-fragile. The most contemporary example I have was touched on in the previous chapter: the driverless car. When one part of the system undergoes stress, the whole system gets stronger. However, as humankind has gone through stages of cultural and organisational evolution, we've tended to create scale by increasing control and mitigating risk,. I think we've made our systems more and more fragile. Take the traditional education system for example. Kids are shepherded through a very precise timetable, into different rooms, in very controlled environments where they passively receive information until they go on to a more *grown-up* version of the same thing which culminates in the world of work, which is typically the same. In these systems people are protected from randomness and uncertainty, which is ridiculous in a complex and exponentially changing world. An anti-fragile version of this system would expose the students to far more randomness, not so much randomness that it is unsafe, but enough randomness that the students grow from exposure to very frequent but small amounts of stress. Hence the development of more and more *challenge based* or *project based* schools where the children own their own education and grow through trial and error, as much if not more than they do through didactic pedagogy.

So this intentional exposure to small stressors is a key part of anti-fragility. This isn't to say we must expose the whole system to constant stress, that would risk breakdown, but by allowing small parts of the system to experience different stresses at different times, we allow the whole system to grow. I think of it as *spreading your bets*, or as Nassim Taleb far more eloquently puts it *"optionality"*. This links back to the Single Point Of Failure metaphor I gave earlier with technology. Currently because our governments tend to be highly centralised, it is dangerous to expose the system to too much stress and randomness because the whole system could break. In more distributed systems however, we are able to expose different sections to different stresses in order for the whole system to learn. Think of it as a constant R&D lab. The good ideas will make it through the entire system if they make it through trial and error. The bad ones will die.

Now there are of course examples of this in our political landscapes, I'm not suggesting that startup mentality doesn't exist, I'm just suggesting we make it systemic.

Make it a part of *the way things are* until we learn that that's not the way things are anymore. A good example of this, as Nassim Taleb describes, is the example of Switzerland.

Switzerland's cantons

Switzerland is possibly the closest thing we have to a direct democracy. The cantons (member states of the Swiss Confederation) have a lot of control over their territory, and central government is run in a more collaborative manner. Whilst there is a president for instance, in reality the role is one of a chairperson for a group of eight people. The head of state is the eight people, not the president. The idea is that with each canton having more control, they can implement things far closer to their needs. Kind of like a smaller and far less radical version of the example of Buurtzorg we gave earlier, who put each unit of 12 of nurses in control in their huge distributed organisation.

Some believe that this heightened control of the cantons is part of the reason why Switzerland has managed to have innovative breakthroughs with policies related to drug abuse for instance, but it is also believed by some to be one important reason why Switzerland is *recession proof*. Because each canton operates slightly differently it also means that the whole system doesn't have a Single Point Of Failure, there is no single domino that can make all others topple. In business terms, this is similar to *diversifying* into other areas, i.e. if our core business eventually fails us, it's ok because we have other areas that keep us strong. The system finds natural equilibrium and is far less volatile. Or rather, is far less volatile far more frequently because of the constant stressors the system learns from. Graphically, I think this would look something like this:

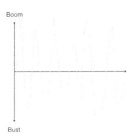

Centralised, fragile system
High and constant volatility, stagnant trajectory

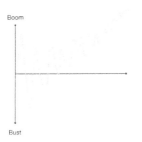

Distributed, anti-fragile system
Low volatility, volatility decreases over time, trajectory increases exponentially due to accumulation, gains from disorder

A Swiss colleague of mine gave me a concrete example of this 'learning nation' in action. He told me the story of Platzspitz in Zürich in the early 80s. If you Google the word Platzspitz you'll find loads of images of what seems like a huge squat. It is a spot behind main station, where 1,000-5,000 *"junkies"* would be at any given time. It was a park for heroin, prostitution...etc. Addicts from around Switzerland, Germany, Austria, France would go there, it was a kind of famous mecca underworld.

This was a problem across Switzerland, but Platzspitz was a symbol for what was becoming known as an epidemic. So the local government took action leading to a turning point in Swiss drug policy. They created a 4 pillar strategy:

- ***Prevention*** *(which some believe to have been more PR than anything else)*
- ***Repression*** *(no more open drug scene, police got enforced, Platzpitz got walled, every time an open drug scene popped up the police would clean it)*
- ***Damage reduction*** *(tried to make it less harmful to consume drugs by opening rooms where they could take less damaging alternatives like methadone for example)*
- ***Therapy*** *(services to help rehabilitate addicts)*

This was a local prototype, and the result was that Zurich took control of the drug system. There is no such thing as a national drug policy. This success story was at least partly adopted in other cantons in Switzerland enabling the whole country to learn from this case. This is made possible by the different layers that Switzerland operates on when it comes to the devolution and decentralisation of power. For instance:

- National system decides: What drugs you can and cannot take. E.g. tobacco is ok
- Local system decides: How do we help with the problem. E.g. In some cities you can smoke in a separated room, in others you can't smoke in a restaurant at all
- Administrations play the roles of links between local, canton, citizen
- These mandates between levels are always changing.

Sound familiar? This partly distributed model follows some of the principles of Sociocracy (to be clear, it isn't a Sociocracy, but it is a highly devolved type of direct democracy) with administrators linking between concentric circles so that the system can remain dynamic and continue to change and evolve. The benefit of the feedback loops created between these different cells on organisational and national levels is very well summed up by Matthew Syed in his book, *'Black Box Thinking: The Surprising Truth About Success'*:

> *The failure of companies in a free market, is not a defect of the system, or an unfortunate byproduct of competition; rather, it is an indispensable aspect of any evolutionary process. According to one economist, 10% of American companies go bankrupt every year. The economist Joseph Schumpeter called this 'creative destruction'.*

> *Now, compare this with centrally planned economies, where there are almost no failures at all. Companies are protected from failure by subsidy. The state is protected from failure by the central bank's printing press, which can inflate its way out of trouble. At first, this may look like an enlightened way to go about solving the problems of economic production, distribution and exchange. Nothing ever fails and, by implication, everything looks successful.*

> *But this is precisely why planned economies didn't work. They were manned by intelligent planners who decided how much grain to produce, how much iron to mine, and who used complicated*

calculations to determine the optimal solutions. (...)

Even if the planners were 10 times smarter than the businessmen operating in a market economy, they would still fall way behind. Without the benefit of a valid test, the system is plagued by rigidity. In markets, on the other hand, it is the thousands of little failures that lubricate and, in a sense, guide the system. When companies go under, other entrepreneurs learn from these mistakes, the system creates new ideas, and consumers ultimately benefit.

I don't think it's mad to assert that the United States, the home of free market economics, also benefits from some level of anti-fragility from the devolved state system.

Some less legal examples from the internet: anti-fragile on steroids!

Being distributed and decentralised in its very nature, the internet is the perfect system to apply anti-fragile thinking to. The best examples of this are probably from piracy. The most famous example of this is The Pirate Bay, an illegal (now, in most countries) peer-to-peer torrenting website allowing anybody to download almost any files for free.

With obvious copyright issues, the founders of The Pirate Bay were eventually arrested by the authorities, but since then the site hasn't been down for a single day. Why? Because every time a Pirate Bay website gets taken down, another one pops up somewhere else on the internet, there are hundreds of them. Online, once the genie is let out of the bottle, you can't put it back in, it just keeps spreading and replicating. Like when you cut a worm in two, you just get two worms. The same is valid for Popcorn Time, another torrenting platform specifically for movies. This platform offers a front-end user experience similar to Netflix whilst the back-end is a peer-to-peer torrent network much like Pirate Bay. Again, every time it gets taken down in one place it pops up somewhere else. The thing that makes this possible is open code. Because the code is available online, anybody can use it anywhere and once it's online of course it can't really be taken down.

I'm not advocating copyright infringement here (though I do think they're an awesome bunch of digital revolutionaries), I'm simply using these examples to highlight two things:
- *We can intentionally build systems to gain from disorder*
- *There is a clear lack of understanding of internet logic by the institutions which govern us*

Rather than fight something that replicates at great speed like a game of 'whack-a-mole', our governing institutions must learn to adopt anti-fragile thinking to build structures fit to evolve rather than hold us back. This is perhaps why the West has struggled to fight terrorism so much. Terrorist cells don't operate in the same way as our armies. They have little central authority and because of their ideological foundations, even taking down the kingpin (e.g. Bin Laden) can cause another cell to pop up somewhere else, sometimes in a different form (e.g. ISIS).

Derisking by spreading our bets

The problem is that in our current political landscapes, we have a say very rarely (elections every four years for instance), on very indirect things (e.g. choosing a party which chooses the policy), which are very centralised (e.g. central government is very far away), with very few options (e.g. UK / EU referendum was simple 'in' or 'out'). A highly fragile state to be in.

Let us imagine for a minute what a mathematically more antifragile system might look like. Let's spread our bets. The following points are principles for decision making and popular involvement in social issues which I think would lead us towards a more distributed, less volatile, anti-fragile and prosperous system. Here's my little thought experiment...

Frequency

In our normal political system we tend to vote every general election which is normally around every 4 years, and in the odd referendum which don't come along too often. If populations voted on things which affected them very directly, it is possible for them to vote very frequently on small but very concrete topics. There are loads of benefits to this. Voting more often would mean no decision is forever (test & learn) but also, it would hopefully engage people far more in the running of their communities because they would be regularly having an impact and in more direct ways.

What could this look like?
For instance, it could be possible that every single day the population gets to vote on a device to make a decision about a topic. This could vary from the way we are governed, to decisions in their community, to how resources are split across different areas. With technology like Blockchain we are able to reduce the risk of voting being hacked or corrupted which makes this far more likely to succeed. We'll see this in the examples of Democracy Earth and MiVote in the next part.

Iteration

Related to frequency is iteration. In our classic political system the decisions we make are there to stay for a while. When we vote in a political party, we are then ruled by that party for a certain period of time. If we had a more organic process where we vote for policies, not parties, we might benefit from the ability to trial new initiatives in small pockets.

Iteration and dynamism would be in all parts of this system. Not only would policies be iterated on and therefore able to improve, but we would also iterate on bigger things like 'deciding how we decide'. A dynamic and constantly changing set of guidelines about how we govern ourselves would make for a system which is always moving and improving because of the tangible changes made by real people not politicians. It would be very difficult to be a career politician with this system in place because to create change you would have to create momentum around real movements for change.

What could this look like?
A certain community may decide to vote on a particular policy that would be unlikely to be adopted across a country by a centralised government (e.g. drug regulation). In a new system, that community would be able to vote to test this for a certain period of time, learn

from that experience and then vote again based on the results from the test. If successful, other communities could easily copy. If not, we revert to the old or try something new. No decision is forever, which means less upheaval and more constant improvements. We'd get to learn from our failures and rectify them quickly to spread all learning to other communities.

Volume

It is sad to see that in major referendums or general elections, there is often a large percentage of people who do not vote. In Australia, voting is compulsory but that isn't always the best way either, as illustrated quite literally by the fact that a significant proportion of the electorate regularly draw penises on their voting cards. There must be many reasons for people not voting including: disengagement, logistical issues (like travel or availability), accessibility, apathy and disbelief, and lack of information.

In system which made better use of technology, decisions could be made far closer to the person voting and could potentially increase engagement and reduce apathy. Being able to vote using technology would also make the process so easy, that more people would be able to vote from wherever they find themselves, anytime. The hope is that with ease of access to political engagement, this would lead to a higher level of knowledge with decisions being increasingly informed over time. We have smartphones now, to think that we have to post our vote or drive to the local school or village hall to put a piece of paper in a box is a bit 1980s.

Directly deciding about policy, not parties or people

Whilst voting for the leader of a country is of course an incredibly important decision, it is still quite far removed from our day to day lives and includes a lot of assumptions. There are issues of trust and assumptions around personality. The same as voting In or Out of a referendum as the UK did with the European Union in 2016. For instance, a person may want to vote 'In' to certain policies but 'Out' of other policies. There are surely more direct ways a person can affect social decisions according to their belief system.

I find it interesting to imagine a situation whereby decisions could be made on policies more than people or parties. With power being distributed across the population, *politics* with its negative connotations of ego and power are reduced, with decisions being made purely about the world we want to live in, tangibly. This distinction between 'policy' and 'parties/people' is possibly the biggest shift that we could envision. It fundamentally changes the way our lives are run. For the first time we have the technology available for true 'direct democracy'.

Transparent

We often know very little about the decisions being made or the people making them. Centralisation often relies on secrecy in order to make decisions without being constantly questioned or judged. That secrecy is the source of power.

In a radically transparent decision making process. All information about policy or process could be available to anybody and anybody could help shape that decision. We are entering an era of accountability, and one of exponential learning where each community could learn from the others all the time. Open data would be a default rather than an exception. And its use would be fundamental to social innovation.

Take a service like CityMapper for instance, an app which allows people to map the best route considering all forms of transport in cities all around the world. That service is only possible because the travel data from trains, buses, trams...etc is open. In a sense what we see here is a situation where open data allows a private company to make something excellent that would normally be provided by substandard public services, with completely different user experiences across the world. Now when I'm in London or Amsterdam or Mexico City or Melbourne I navigate using the same familiar interface, and the anxiety of city travel is removed. All this is made possible because a startup had access to the data.

In summary

We could design a system which reduces risk and volatility and increases prosperity over time by allowing:
- *More people,*
- *to make more decisions,*
- *more often*
- *with more direct impact*
- *and access to more information.*

The idea could be to create a system which constantly adapts, reducing the negative 'bust' moments in economics and social policy. It also means that each decision would carry far less significance in the grand scheme of things. Our vote for who should be president or prime minister at the moment carries huge weight and importance. It isn't something we can afford to take lightly and it is possible to regret this decision. With a distributed, dynamic, direct and highly frequent system, no decision is forever and there are daily opportunities to shape the world we live in.

systems comparison

	Classic system	New system
Proximity	**Indirect democracy** Population decides who decides but not how they decide or what they decide on	**Direct democracy** Population decides how decisions are made, and what decisions are made
Regularity	**Rare** Population rarely gives input such as general elections and occasional referendums	**Constant** There is a constant state of referendum on 'what' decisions are made, 'how' decisions are made
Information	**Selective openness** Information is shared as means to gain trust	**Radical openness** Information is open by default as a premise for systemic learning and informed decision making

Volume	**Few people input** Input into decisions is a static event in time (e.g. election) with barriers to entry (e.g. travel…)	**Many people input** It is easy and accessible for everybody to input
Permanence	**Forever** Decisions are 'final' or at least remain for very long periods of time.	**For now** All decisions are tests with varied testing periods. The learnings are published in order to iterate and continue testing.

In an equation,
what might this look like?

I'm definitely not a mathematician, but this is a useful thought experiment to imagine what it might look like. The lower the number is, the higher volatility is and the higher impact each decision has on the entire system. The higher the number, the lower the volatility is because each decision or intervention represents a small percentage of the total interventions made.

volatility calculation = #of people x #of decisions x #of communities

New system equation:
Assumptions made are: a community of 1000 people, voting 365 days per year, with 100 communities of 10 people, voting once per per day (for instance)

New system volatility = 1000 x 365 x 100 = 36,500,000

Classic system equation:
Assumptions made are: a community of 1000 people, voting once every 4 years with 10 communities of 100 people

Classic political system volatility = 1000 x 0.25 x 10 =

2,500

Comparison:

36,500,000 / 2,500 = 14,600

This is all a bit of fun of course, but using this calculation, we could contemplate a system which is 14,600 times less volatile than the classic political system.

The bad will die, the good will spread

The flaw in this equation (one of many I'm sure), is that it only calculates the diminished risk. What it doesn't do is show the amount of opportunity that comes from these many many decisions. In a system where many many decentralised decisions are being made in small pockets, the bad decisions aren't as likely to spread, and the good ones are likely to spread like a virus or meme. In the same way that startups move faster than big corporates, this system could allow this process to occur on a social level.

"You never change things by fighting the existing reality. To change something, build a new model that makes the existing model obsolete."

Richard Buckminster Fuller

part 3: stories from the frontline

So far we've explored different influences, trends, methodologies and philosophies from the worlds of technology, organisational design and business to construct a broad picture of the new factors which will no doubt play a part in the future of governance. If nothing else, I hope this book so far shows just how unfit our current system is for the world we live in. Now I'd like to get concrete and suggest real alternatives to the existing system. This isn't anything new and it isn't something I've made up. There are real initiatives attacking this topic from all sorts of different angles and having powerful impacts on the communities they're working with.

During my research I've been humbled again and again as I've spoken to some incredibly inspiring people. People with enormous ambitions to change the systems through which we are governed. They will now become our protagonists as we dive into the detail and into the real. I'll introduce you to our new friends in a minute, but first a little about the process I went through.

I reached out to the founders of each of these initiatives on social media, either directly approaching them or through mutual contacts or even friends of friends of friends (I love networked society). Once in touch with them, I spoke with each of our stars for up to two hours each on Skype. The interviews were quite informal with only a broad outline and a strong intention to hear about the reality of what they are 'actually doing' and how they see the future. Abridged versions of these interviews are available by searching 'flux' on your podcast app.

For me it was an amazing journey, and as the interviews progressed, patterns starting forming as if they were all different pieces of the same puzzle.

So let's explore the projects which could be pointing towards the future of democracy. For each story, I will share my summary and takeaways upfront, before letting them tell their story with edited interviews with some commentary around points I found particularly insightful. Enjoy.

MiVote

Key principles
The 'non-ideology' ideology
Destinational democracy
Informed electorate
Hybrid decision making
Transparency

"There is no excuse in 2016, when you can have a many-to-many and any-to-one conversation, that we do not have a conversation with our electorate on every issue. There is just simply no excuse for it."

Adam Jacoby

MiVote in a nutshell

Worried about his children's future and angry at the diminishing level of citizen participation in politics, Australian entrepreneur Adam Jacoby decided to stop moaning on Twitter and do something about it. The result is the application of startup thinking and critical enquiry to a broken democratic system: MiVote.

> *"MiVote is a blockchain enabled digital platform that is intending to the most genuinely democratic political model that exists in the world today."*

It was recently a finalist in the Grand Global Challenge Award at the Singularity University's Global Innovation Summit (founded by the famous Ray Kurzweil, mentioned earlier).

Why is this interesting?

The 'non-ideology' ideology: if the role of government is to 'enact the will of the people', it is an irony to even have party ideologies, as they represent the will of the party, not the people. This is why MiVote doesn't take any political stance. It asks the people what they want and helps them to make their decision in an informed way.

Destinational democracy: voting on policies, or parties/

politician makes very little sense if we don't first align on where we're going. MiVote's 'destinational democracy' is an innovative concept that can help unite citizens around common directions and result in policies in line with a shared vision.

Informed electorate: giving citizens more direct input into how their nations run relies on the electorate being better informed than it has been previously. This brings up the question of whether it is even possible to be truly well informed but this is something MiVote have thought of. Their independent researchers compile different frames to see policy decisions through and require the electorate to engage with that information before being able to vote.

Hybrid decision making: to combat the dualistic and binary voting system, MiVote adopts a ranking system during voting similar to the Single Transferable Vote but with the spirit of consent decision making. This means that we vote for what we can tolerate, resulting in less disenfranchisement.

Transparent: MiVote doesn't accept any corporate or interest group funding at all. It is entirely individual-donation funded. They don't accept company money, but if the CEO of a company wants to write a cheque in their own name, they will accept that. All on the proviso that they understand the donation will be made public on the website with both their name and the amount, and that they're getting no access whatsoever to the policy and research teams. There is a complete disconnect between the people who are putting the frames together, and any access to the donating group.

MiVote
in their own words

A Democratic Enterprise

Inspired by the concept and curious to hear the full story, I asked Adam to tell me a little bit about his background:

MiVote was percolating away in the back of my brain from about 5 years ago I suppose. That was a time when I'd decided to take a very short break from running businesses. I'm about the only one in my family without a PhD... I didn't go to university... I started my first business when I got out of high school, and my father was begging me for years to "just get a degree" because "this crazy entrepreneurship stuff won't work one day" and I'd need to have something to "fall back on".

So after a few businesses, I decided I'd take a year off and go to university and I started with a Masters in Entrepreneurship and Innovation, *and that's what really had me starting to think about how to reach a number of people in a significant way. I was learning about all the things they teach in business school and entrepreneur school around business casing and cut-through and mitigating risk and understanding risk and all the boring stuff they teach that is actually reasonably useless.*

But the idea of MiVote seemed to keep nagging in the back of Adam's brain until...

I started thinking about doing things above and beyond money. Shortly thereafter, my first child was born - I have 4 kids - and I was becoming increasingly despondent about the fact that my children's voices were becoming less and less relevant as every day went by. All I was seeing, in Australia at least - and I have a fairly significant interest in US politics because I lived in the US for a long time - was about a system that was fundamentally broken. It was becoming less accessible for the average person to have a voice that meant anything, there was more and more validation about this idea that in fact the correlation between the will of the people and legislation was growing further and further apart. The average policy just didn't have any relevance to what was going on in the world. I didn't really want my children to grow up in a world where that was the case, and they were just bystanders to the decisions that would affect their lives. I sat down with my father and a couple of other people that I'm close to… some mentors and I thought, "I can sit here and snipe on Twitter from the background and talk about how terrible politics is for the majority of people, or I can actually try and do something about it."

And so like any good entrepreneur, he did…

So I spent some time thinking about democracy as though it were a business, a startup. If democracy is the product, what does the market want and what does the market need? Because we've reached this point in time where it doesn't serve its customers anymore, and for it to do the job that it was originally intended to do, it really needs to be redesigned. So that's how the whole thing started.

I started pitching it people to see if it resonated and made sense, and didn't offend too much. I don't mean offend ideologically, I mean offend logically. I'm fortunate to have a lot of friends who are judges and former judges, and politicians and former politicians and community leaders and business leaders. The more I went out to talk to people in that first year after I had started framing it - I must have spoken to 100 people about it - and the sense was that "it's not perfect yet, but you're onto something". *It kept building and building and shaping and then I introduced it to a group of people who I invited into the project and it's just gone crazy from there!*

So what beliefs underpin MiVote?

MiVote is a blockchain enabled digital platform that is intending to, and is building what we believe is the most genuinely democratic political model that exists in the world today. I say that without in any way wanting to disrespect my fellow democratic innovators around the world, some of whom you've already spoken to - and some of the people you've spoken to I have an existing relationship with - Pia Mancini is the rockstar of our movement right now (you'll meet her cofounder Santi later on in the book). *We're all approaching these challenges in different ways and we all have enormous mutual respect for one another because there is a genuine intent to make the world we live in a better place for more people. We just view it in a slightly different way.*

MiVote is about creating a representative movement (like Democracy Earth which we'll cover later), *we will run candidates in the Australian senate at the next federal election, and most likely a couple of state elections before we reach the federal election. But we start from a very different place that everybody else does. We start from a thought that genuine democracy doesn't actually exist anywhere in the world at the moment. There are people that are trying to create it, but at the moment it doesn't exist. It doesn't exist because fundamentally, democracy is about the enactment of the will of the people. When I put the 'Australia lens' over this, we can't have democracy there is no way that the government or the opposition could claim to be enacting the will of the people, because they never ask people what they actually want! If you're not engaged in a dialogue with your constituency, it's impossible to deliver the outcome that the majority of people want. If we were going to drill down into the reality of it, it would be near impossible for either our prime minister, or the leader of the opposition, to confidently validate that they even understand what the electorate want.*

We start from a place that says there is a dialogue, which is obvious, and there are a lot of other

groups like Democracy Earth and others around the
world, who are doing that. And we start from a
place that says that we don't have a policy position
until our constituency has spoken, and we have a
majority position. But that's where we start to divert
from the others.

Our first starting place is that ideology is the single
largest threat to democracy on the planet. It's a
threat for a couple of reasons. Having a political
ideologically fundamentally says "I have an answer
to the question before you've even asked it,
because my worldview shapes my thinking about
every issue." *I give speeches about democracy*
quite a bit around the world, a lot in Australia, and I
start every conversation with the same question to
the audience, "do you believe that there's any
worldview or ideology that genuinely has the
solution for every problem that faces us as a
people/nation?" *Invariably, everybody in the*
audience says no, and yet what our adversarial,
binary political system requires, is for us to vote for
a party on the basis that it will make all the right
decisions on our behalf, with a thought or idea that
we vote for them because we know what they're
going to do or alternatively, they know what we
want. That's simply not the case; an election does

not a democracy make.

The Destinational Perspective

The main interpretation I've pulled out of this case, which is key to the thinking in this book, is that the strongest held ideology that Adam and MiVote hold is to 'not have any ideologies'. That is to say, they aren't advocating a particular political decision, they're trying to provide the framework in which the people can express their will. This is why I have tried not to discuss the 'content' of any political decisions in much detail in this book, because this isn't about the content of these decisions but about the process by which these decisions are made. We'll talk about ideology shortly but first I wanted to hear Adam talk about the key differentiator in MiVote's process, which is that they start by looking at the 'where-to'. In other words, the destination that the country wants to go in. Adam very eloquently calls this a 'destinational frame' and puts it like this:

> *We start from a place that says that we do not have any ideological position and we're not wedded to any solution that might exist for any issue. What we've done is decoupled the binary legislative conversation from democracy and replaced it with a conversation about destination. So rather than*

saying, "Do you support the bill? Yes or No? Right, we've got enough Yes's, that's where the party/the movement is going" *We actually say,* "no, we want to talk about the destination. Where do you as an individual, and we collectively as a country/ citizenry want our government and our country to go?"

We present 4 different destinational frames that our constituency can vote for. So for example, if you look at the immigration issue which is obviously a significant issue everywhere in the world at the moment, because it tends to couple itself with asylum seekers as an issue. What we have now in Australia (Brexit in the UK is a good example) is a situation where we talk about the care that is required of asylum seekers and how many should we bring in and so forth.

The problem is that that conversation is already tied to the particular worldviews of the two major political parties who for the most part are actually identical in their thinking. There is no real choice for the electorate the think about what is an alternative worldview. So on the immigration issue as an example, the kind of things that we would do with our constituency... the vote would be, "would you like the government, the country, to take a primarily 'humanitarian' approach to asylum seekers or immigration? Would you like it to take 'security' approach? Would you like it to take a 'financially pragmatic' approach? Or would you like it to take an 'international diplomacy' approach?" *The question is a different question because you're actually talking about where you want us to go.*

It's a long-term question, as opposed to "do you support this particular bill or not?" *Because one of the challenges we have with the ideological, adversarial system that exists today is that the conversations are always pitches - we are being pitched to all the time without any conversation about what that particular pitch does and where it takes us in the long term. Brexit's a good example of a whole load of people who made a vote on the basis of a short-term conversation, but get to the end of that conversation and go,* "you know what, I really didn't understand what it meant" *or* "I wasn't aware that these were the exact outcomes that would happen" *and that's not for everybody because some people were very aware and very informed. But certainly, what I'm reading, is that there were a lot of people who only understood part of the issue.*

Around the time I was editing my conversation with Adam, I stumbled across an excerpt from a UK radio interview on LBC which makes this point incredibly well. The radio show host James O'Brien, asked his interviewee to describe why he voted out of the EU in the Brexit referendum. That person said:

> *"I was willing to take that sacrifice* (short term financial loss as a result of the Out decision) *just for the independence and so we control our own laws."*

James O'Brien goes on to ask his guest:

> *"Which law is it you're really looking forward to not having to obey anymore?"*

The interviewee had no answer. He couldn't list a single law, let alone one he wanted to get rid of. This is an information issue, which we will address in a minute, but it is also a question around the framing of the decision. Rather than vote 'In' or 'Out', MiVote suggests that we vote together as to the kind of country we want to be in the future. MiVote begins the conversation with a destinational frame.

Another benefit of this destinational perspective can be

illustrated by this model (which I think I've adapted from Peter Senge's Fifth Discipline over the years) I often share with groups of executives in regards to decision making and why it's important to align around a more holistic perspective before agreeing on the nitty gritty details. Specifically, aligning around a vision of the future helps conversations to be more constructive as we all move in the same direction:

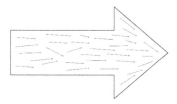

Alignment

We all work in a direction, we start by aligning on holistic topics (e.g. principles, values, vision), we focus on 'where to' and 'how' before 'what', momentum is kept up.

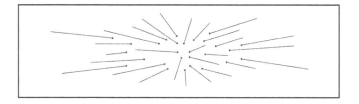

Agreement

We go straight into the details before agreeing where we're going or why we'd doing it. Energy is drained from crossing conversations going around in circles.

A no ideology ideology

I was also interested by this idea that all decisions are clouded by the ideologies of political parties. I was keen to know more about the 'no ideology ideology'. To be more specific, MiVote doesn't adhere to a particular ideology but it does have a set of pretty fundamental human values that it follows. Adam says:

> *Everything we do is underpinned with our value set and the value set of MiVote is not negotiable. If the majority of MiVote constituents said "we want a border security approach - a more right-leaning approach to the immigration issue" even that would still have to be vetted to some degree by the value set. The value set is meritocracy, equality of opportunity, transparency, accountability and ideas like that. We won't create, endorse or support policy that will harm people or disadvantage people on the basis of their race or their religion. But if the majority says that they want to protect the borders then that is the position that the movement will take.*

So the value set acts as a kind of ethical firewall, a fundamentally evil policy could never be passed under the MiVote process, because it would contravene the fundamental values. Adam went on to give an example of a topic that is very close to him personally and how he would have to deal with that if a decision he strongly disagreed with were taken by the constituency:

> *I have a number of friends who are gay and I'm very close with them, I'm invested in their lives, their very close with my wife and my children, and my Dad said* "so let's say for example that MiVote is really successful and you get a million members to the movement and you get representatives in parliament and you ask the people about marriage equality, and let's say the movement doesn't support marriage equality but you personally really believe in it, obviously, because you have a context, you have relationships with people, you have friends for whom this is a really important issue".

> *I couldn't answer the question at the beginning. I had to go away for a few days and really meditate on that question and how would I feel about being involved with a movement that fundamentally advocated and fought for a position I didn't believe in. And where I got to on the meditation was that if that's what happens when a group of citizens have an opportunity to see a variety of different options*

and are informed about what each of those options are, well that's democracy. You win some and you lose some. Just because I want it, it doesn't mean that it should happen.

An informed constituency

MiVote don't take a stance, they just ensure that the decisions made by citizens are as informed as possible. This is another pillar of MiVote which answers one of the questions that has come up most by people I've shared my research with. The question of informed decision making. How can we help our political contributions to be better informed? Can we ever truly be well informed? Should uninformed people be allowed to vote at all?

The answers to these questions aren't easy. My first answer when naysayers or cynics ask this question in response to the idea of a deeper democracy, is that it wouldn't be difficult to improve on our existing system which is essentially propaganda based. You need only look at the 2016 US elections, at several examples of misinforming the public during Brexit (from both sides), false claims of weapons of mass destruction which led to the 2003 Iraq War or countless examples of propaganda in the past.

It's difficult to share accurate or objective information, it's really difficult to have people engage with this information, and it is even harder to help it be understood without including bias (whether by design or accident). Nonetheless, MiVote takes an important stance in improving this. Adam is pretty clear that this isn't the case:

We have a 'warts-and-all' approach to that. One of my very first conversations when I started this movement, was with an old friend who was a former judge and we had this argument about "is there such thing as truth and what is truth?" *and he was arguing that there's no such thing as truth and again if you use the immigration argument, there are no facts, there is no such thing as facts. And that's absolute bullshit because there absolutely are facts, the problem is that the public don't have access to most of them.*

We would say that there are facts to support all sides and all destinations, but what you get is a collection of facts pitched to you for a particular purpose, for a particular worldview, without acknowledging that there are also facts that are inconvenient, that might lend themselves to a different worldview.

Because we're not advocating for any one position, all we want is for all of that to see the light of day. We want to inundate you with information (I don't mean that in an oppressive way so that no-one's actually going to do it)... we want to provide you with enough information that you need to be able to make decision that's informed without in any way suggesting to you that you should feel a particular way about the facts that are provided. So in the case of immigration: for good and for bad and for everything inbetween, these are the realities - this is how many people came in by boat, this is how many people died at sea, this is how much it costs to process somebody offshore, this is what it costs to process somebody onshore, this is whether or not the law contravenes the legal definition required by international treaties... etc ... These are black and white things, it's not interpretation.

This is how MiVote attempts to tackle this problem:

The first peg in the ground for us is that the majority position always rules - the majority creates the policy. The second peg in the ground is - we are non-ideological. We're going to provide you with a suite of destinational options so that you can understand the issue and understand that you have choice. The third peg in the ground is that you can't have genuine democracy without an informed constituency. If what we have is (I think this is the case... it's certainly the case in the US, when I lived there, and it's the case absolutely in Australia) these media propaganda machines that provide information and the data that supports their worldview, completely ignoring the data that might not support their view, what you have is a constituency who is unable to make an informed decision.

They're voting for things that they don't understand, or that they're misinformed about because they've deliberately been provided with misinformation. A big part about the investment in our movement is in research, and objective researchers. What we do is to provide quite a detailed frame of reference for what each of those destinations might look like. So if you take the immigration example that I provided you, the user experience would be this:

1. You download the app for nothing - so you're now a member - it costs you nothing, we push notify you and say:

2. "We're having the immigration policy vote on Friday, do you want to opt in to that vote?" *Yes I do - click the button.*

3. At that point, your personal library in your app will fill with the information related to that issue. When you go into that library, you'll then be able to look at each of the frames. It will say, "if you believed in a humanitarian approach, these are the things you would believe in, these are the positions you couldn't support, these are the current parties that that position aligns to at the moment" *and you can delve as deeply as you want into it.*

So there's the short-term, dot-point precis version of understanding the issue. If you go, "that's interesting but I don't have enough information to know if that's really what I believe and that's the destination I want the country to take." *Then you can press cascade down and you'll go into a 4 or 5 page overview which has been written by our researchers.*

If that's not enough, you can cascade further and then have access to all the links to all of the source documentation and reports that helped formulate the frames. So you can go as deeply as you like into the information and the issues.

4. And then we ask you to vote. The vote will come up.

5. The results of the vote are available 48 hours after the vote takes place to all of our members, and then shortly thereafter to the media, because that's what forms policy position.

Breaking the user experience down shows such a simplicity that it perplexes me that this isn't already the case. It's as simple as 1,2,3 (4,5).

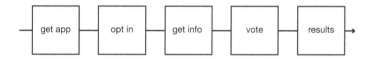

He went on to say...

It's populist to some degree, but my discomfort is that the word 'populist' has been hijacked in our political discourse as being a negative.

But that is what democracy is about. What it misses in the current frame, and what we are trying to fix, is that the populist view is also the informed view.

So when I said that you have your own library, the way that our digital mechanism works is that if you opt into the immigration conversation vote, and you never open your library, your voting light will never go on. If you don't choose to be informed, we choose not to listen to you. So that's a pretty fundamental difference to what everybody else is doing.

Objective Information

But how do you make sure this is objective information and not your just your biased worldview?

We have four governance protocols within our process that work towards objectivity, so it's not like somebody can sit in a room and put a frame together, a destination, and just whack it up on the website. It has to go through the policy committee, then the ethics committee, then the governance committee, and then it has to be signed off by the council which is our board. So there are four checks and balances to make sure that we are not advocating for anything, and that the positions that are put forward provide as much information as is readily available that we can get our hands on. That's point A.

Then point B, for each of the potential destinations actually we provide some information that contextualises it.. that's real, that's factual, that's not speculation, it's not hearsay… it is what is. If you look at things like climate change and you have scientists who believe one thing and scientists who believe another. We would highlight the fact that there are a group of scientists who believe this, but that group is the minority, and here are the groups and members and associations and universities who have a particular view.

So we're not saying you shouldn't listen to all views, we're actually encouraging you to understand what everybody is saying and make a determination for yourself, on the weight of evidence, what you think makes the most sense.

Pit stop summary:

You can't vote if you don't read a minimum of research before hand. So, in terms of the MiVote framework we now have:

- Destinational? Check.
- Informed? Check.

What of the issue that democracy is inherently divisive, in that it's predicated on majorities and minorities and that the slightest of margins can allow one group to rule over another? Well MiVote have thought of that too and have taken some measures to improving upon the existing system. They do this through consent based decision making and the single transferable vote.

Point C for us is that we don't have a 51-49% majority as most binary, legislative E-voting platforms do. The nature of our proprietary voting system is that we get to 60%. When we say the majority of our constituents want something, we genuinely mean the majority. We're not talking about 49/51 and so the party and the movement is divided. We actually say, really genuinely, most of the people want this as a direction. And once that direction has been set, unlike the binary yes and no of a legislation conversation, then our representatives in the senate have a constitutional requirement (under our constitution) to represent that position of our constituency.

So whoever is writing the bill, whether it's this current government or the government from the next election, our representative's responsibility is to only make a determination if it delivers to the destination that the majority of our people want. There's a negotiating nuance in there that allows us to try and make it more closely aligned, but still be pragmatic and understand that no issue is just black and white. Most people don't just want humanitarian, or just want border security, they want a little bit of everything. The way that our system works is that we're able to analyse through the voting mechanism, not just what the most successful frame of reference is, but then in order, what the next three look like as well. So we have a sense of what's most and least important to our constituency and that then becomes part of the negotiation.

What I find in this element is that what MiVote are doing seems like a combination the idea of consent based decision making with the single transferable voting system to make rapid consent available on a mass scale. This is to say, that you rank for the things that are 'within your range of tolerance'. The desired outcome is not only that the final decision is more representative but also that the likelihood of a decision that is outside of the population's range of tolerance is very low. So the worst situation is avoided for the most.

I also wanted to know more from Adam in terms of the financial side of things and corruption and power more broadly. As we discussed in PART 1, the way candidates are currently funded is a huge part of the system, as is career politics. This was Adam's response:

> We don't accept any corporate or interest group funding at all. So this is entirely, individual-funded, donor funded. So if you want to give us money as a company, we won't accept it, but if the CEO of a company wants to write a cheque in their own name, we will accept that, on the proviso that they understand that: a) that donation will be made public on the website with both their name and the amount, and that's not negotiable, and b) that they're getting no access whatsoever to the policy and research teams. So there's a complete disconnect between the people who are putting the frames together, and any access to the donating group, which is really important.

We've also stripped back some of that empire-building political ambition - under our constitution, you can't serve more than two terms as a representative if you were to be elected. This isn't about you becoming prime minister, this isn't about you trying to build a name for yourself.

Part of the condition is that you come in understanding that you will at times have to advocate for a majority of positions that you personally may not believe in at all, and so you have two terms as a civic duty rather than as an ability for you to build your own profile. Then you have a requirement under our constitution, to mentor the next generation of representatives as they come through.

In conclusion

The MiVote story is staggering to me in its sheer robustness. They seem to have covered almost every base, and can serve as exemplars of every principle that I've explored and advocated in this book.

To summarise this chapter, here is a reminder of the different points which make MiVote so special:

The 'non-ideology' ideology
MiVote enacts the will of the people, not its own beliefs.

Destinational democracy
Deciding where we want to go before the deciding the policy.

Informed electorate
Citizens can only vote once they have engaged with the data.

Hybrid decision making
Citizens vote within their range of tolerance, using the single transferable vote method to integrate nuance.

Transparency
It is crowdfunded by individuals and all funding information is made public.

MiVote is a truly staggering example of how democracy can be re-designed by entrepreneurship, not politics (as you'll see become a trend in the following stories). Perhaps this indicates that there is a broader social shift happening.

MiVote is now globally recognised and awarded. It is in demand in 22 countries around the world and I think gives us a clear signpost towards the immediate future of direct informed democracy. The reason I say 'immediate' is because through thorough research into the very foundations of democracy, we've seen that by adding an entrepreneurial desire to really understand what the customer (in this case citizen) wants, and by adding cutting edge tech, MiVote is doing something that is simply logical and almost inevitable for the world we live in today.

With a level of articulation which characterises him, Adam put it like this:

> *"There is no excuse in 2016, when you can have a many-to-many and a many-to-one conversation, that we do not have a conversation with our electorate on every issue. There is just simply no excuse for it."*

Icelandic Crowdsourced Constitution

Key principles

Citizen centricity

Deliberative democracy

Representatives as facilitators

Qualitative constitutional approach

"When we finally get this constitution passed, I know a few people that could say to their grandchildren, "you see this article here in the constitution, I influenced that." I took part in writing the reactions to the internet clause and I have a few words in the bill, so if it gets passed as the constitution, I could tell my daughter that "your father actually wrote these words in the constitution bill". That is quite powerful.

Finnur Magnusson

The Icelandic Crowdsourced Constitution in a nutshell

Born out of the collapse of the Icelandic financial system, entrepreneurs, technologists and creatives around the country gathered unofficially to figure out how to build a better future for their country. The decision and subsequent project was to crowdsource an understanding of the country they would like to be by creating the world's first crowdsourced constitution.

The Icelandic Crowdsourced Constitution is an amazing example of how mass citizen participation can be made possible using in-person workshops, social media, and online mass collaboration processes. There is a twist in this story though, a worrying display of political power plays and the meeting of the old and new world as we transition from powerful people to powerful processes.

Using design thinking and agile methodology, borrowing tools from world famous design process experts like IDEO, the team behind the constitution created divergent and convergent phases to listen to the people, prototype, ship and get feedback from citizens. This iterative process meant releasing new versions of the constitution on a weekly basis involving over 40,000 people in the process.

Why is this interesting?

Citizen centricity: enacting the will of the people requires listening to them in the first place. This process was radical in doing so. Through workshops with 1,000 citizens, online deliberation and feedback, the document was a result of constant iteration based on the people's needs.

Deliberative democracy: an argument against direct democracy is that democracy without deliberation remains simplistic and binary. Whilst deliberation happens naturally in pubs and on social media, this process actively sought deliberation and feedback online to promote discussions which would result in a tighter and more representative constitution for everybody.

Representatives as facilitators: the role of representatives still isn't clear in these new models but the Icelandic process offers us an example of how things could be. In this process, representatives were facilitators. Their role was to listen to people's needs and help articulate them in a way that moved the nation forward, rather than remaining stuck in combative debate.

Qualitative constitutional approach: Whilst MiVote and Democracy Earth mostly use voting mechanisms, this process is impressive in its ability to integrate multiple views (over 40,000) from complex verbal and written data. An incredible feat really, and with language processing technology getting more and more sophisticated, this could become even better in the future.

The Icelandic Constitution in their own words

This is possibly the most famous example of evolved democracy and citizen participation the world has ever seen. Following the country's dramatic financial crisis of 2008, some Icelandic citizens started an incredibly ambitious attempt at neo-democracy: to crowdsource a new constitution for the country by allowing anybody to join the process and sharing results with 100% transparency.

The result was a constitution accepted by almost 70% of the nation and deemed by many to be 'enlightened'. Unfortunately the result was also an odd and obvious example of political gaming as the constitution was halted. But with the Pirate Party and other radical movements gaining in power and influence, it seems the world's first crowdsourced constitution could be on its way to being made official.

The Context

I was lucky enough to interview the CTO of this project and unpicked the process, trying to extract the principles and elements which could provide us with some tips and tricks for what the future of governance could look like. We'll take a look at the lessons from an amazing experiment in participative democracy. I've tried sticking to the original wording as much as possible by creating an abridged or sometimes re-ordered transcript of the relevant sections from the interview. So let's start by hearing Finnur Magnusson's angle on the context from which this initiative was born:

My wife and I we had a long distance relationship for the 3 years I lived in the UK. She came out 6 months before we moved back to Iceland and we moved back to Iceland just as the financial crisis was happening.

So, I came back to a very treacherous situation and there were some grassroots movements that were meeting, both planned or sporadically in Iceland. One of them was the Ministry of Ideas *which was a group of likeminded people that were coming from startup companies and maybe had a technology background or something like that. They were interested in how we could quickly get past this financial collapse and reboot the country.*

This movement was a grassroots group of people

that was combined by one of our ministers to set up an event. Iceland has the oldest parliament in the world so Vikings used to gather in Thingvellir, the location of our national parliament, from all over the country and they made the law and they had discussions about the future of the country...etc.

So we wanted to do a big crowdsourcing event around the future vision and values of the country - "how are we going to rebuild Iceland after the financial collapse?"

And here I think are a couple of amazing lessons from this story. Firstly, that true, fundamental, democratic change can emerge out of hardship, and when a country gets a swift kick up the arse from global economic forces.

The second, that it is possible for people to gather not just in protest on the streets but to create real solutions and a genuine alternative. And that this kind of process can result in something that promotes a new, better alternative, not just in revolt against the old. We can trust ordinary citizens en masse to be constructive towards the creation of a better future.

Finnur goes on to explain how this initiative was then adopted by the powers that be:

Later we had a new government and a new prime minister who was very keen on creating a new constitution, so we started work on a new constitution. We'd had the same constitution since we got our independence from the Danish crown in 1918. The current Icelandic constitution is mainly the Danish one so it's written for a monarch, with slight adaptations through the years, but it hasn't changed much. So Iceland never got its own constitution.

Jóhanna Sigurðardóttir - the prime minister at the time - wanted the constitution to come from the people. She was interested in repeating this crowdsourcing event but with focus on the Icelandic constitution, so some of us who took part in the first event were recruited to do another one.

So with the context set and ready for change to happen, for the country to collectively decide on their destiny, they repeated this process. I asked Finnur to explain what this process looked like:

I took part in developing that process and the technology side of inviting 900 people to an auditorium, collecting all of their thoughts live during the event, using online tools to broadcast the crowdsourcing event to the internet, and collecting all of the thoughts into some sort of a comprehensive result.

The 900 people were a truly random sample from all over the country - these people spent one day brainstorming about the constitution. Then after the brainstorm they set up the constitution council, who would take all that information and turn it into the final document, and they needed at CTO and I got volunteered for that position. I was a part of the team that created that process, with the aim to have a truly open and transparent process for writing a constitution in modern day of age, using all the technology available to us. It was a very agile process where we created a method to capture ideas from hundreds of people during a day. All participants were really happy with the outcome of it and we created values for the Icelandic nation that everyone could agree on.

So to summarise and clarify:

1. About 1,000 people in a room to envision the future of Iceland

2. Then, a small council of 25 people crafted

something complete and concrete and representative

3. They iterated with an agile process so the country could comment, input and improve on what that group had done and so it was visible to all

4. The result: no secrets

I asked Finnur to go into the detail of how this process worked:

We sourced inspiration from companies like IDEO and other design thinking policies. We did a sort of interactive process where we came up with a 4 day script where we did small meetings with maybe 20 or 30 people, and we repeated the process numerous times. The idea was to get a totally random sample from the nation and it started out with broad concepts, almost like warm-up/ brainstorming exercises to get vision and values. Everyone thought about "what do you believe to be the values of the Icelandic nation?" *and they wrote down their ideas and went around and you explained your idea.*

Then we had dot voting and things like that, and we had 10 people at each table and each table

*nominated their top ideas, and then we had
runners. So we had 100 tables with 10 people on
them, and we had trained facilitators at each table,
and we had runners that collected all of those
tickets from each table and ran to the computer lab
where we had 20 or 30 people just typing it in as
quickly as they could. We fed that into the system
and we projected a word-cloud at the first 15
minute break.*

*Then there was this amazing moment where people
looked up and saw their words and said* "hey, this
is what we just decided!" *So we went on and
started talking about different themes and working
on more complex ideas and everyone ended up
submitting all of that data. The data was captured
and typed in as we went.*

Just as an example: Honesty - *heiðarleika in
Icelandic, was by far the biggest word in the first
session. Then you had* Respect, Equality, Justice
*and this captured the atmosphere in 2009, one year
after the collapse. People felt betrayed and they
wanted to build a new society based on honesty.*

*Then we talked about themes - where should we
focus our efforts in the next years. It was* education,

employment, the environment, prosperity, sustainability *and* family *as the main themes they wanted to talk about. Then we created a future vision based on this.*

During the meeting, after each session, we had runners coming in, typing in the data and feeding it back into the meeting and also online. So we came up with this structure, it's actually a very nice brainstorming structure. We've done this after these meetings, with Search and Rescue and companies wanting to capture the atmosphere and create a vision for a group of 100-1,000 people.

My main takeaway here is that this isn't new or innovative really. It feels to me like a standard innovation process, one that many facilitators and process consultants will be familiar with in helping organisations come to a 'shared vision'. In fact, it makes me think how there is little to no excuse for ever not doing this, this has been done with post-it notes and flip charts for a long long time, it's now just a bit easier to run it at a larger scale.

I don't say that to take anything away from this project, the opposite in fact. What is clearly innovative (in that it has never been done before on this scale) is the context they did it in: that of politics and governance. What is innovative is the application of evolved organisational and innovation processes to the vision of a nation, and that is incredible.

They used 'agile', 'design thinking', 'facilitation' and other methodologies and techniques which have been developed for decades in businesses, and applied them to something of incredible national importance. They proved that participative methods are highly applicable to shaping our communities and nations. Anyway, I digress, let's go back to Finnur as he elaborates more:

> So it's a pretty innovative process and it's based on a lot of ideas. Design-thinking ideas and brainstorming ideas, but compiled in a flow that works for a very large audience. And we did the same for the constitution, but it's more focused on what the content of the constitution should be. We actually worked with some of the startups in Iceland to do language processing, to distill core content from the copy, from all the tables in the meeting. The themes for the constitution were Equality, Democracy, Honesty, Human-rights, Justice, Respect, and Freedom. Those were the high-level ones from the first session.

> There were some themes that evolved during the

day, for instance, that the constitution should be written in a language that everyone could understand. There was this concern that Icelandic law is not very easy to read for the people, so they wanted the constitution to be written in a language that everyone could understand... that it wasn't a complicated legal document that you needed to have interpreted for you.

And there was a lot of stuff that is not in the current constitution about ownership of natural/national resources. We have a very rich fishing culture and it's a big part of our income, but it's roughly ten families that control all of the fishing quota, and people are saying that this needs to be distributed more equally. We were also talking about access to our big country, access to clean air and clean water. Who owns the natural resources? Is it us, or can it be sold and traded like a commodity? Things like that came through, and were used as a starting point for the basis of the work of the constitution council. It was then elected after this crowdsourcing event.

Having created the basis for a strong constitution they then sought to create a smaller group which would continue to craft this. Which and this poses a few interesting questions I think:

- What more might be possible?
- What can a crowd do and what can't it do?
- What is the role of inte
- rmediaries or representatives, if any?

What more might be possible?

Now, let's not forget that Iceland is an example of something. It is in Finnur's own words 'an experiment'. That is to say that far far more is surely possible and we are at the beginning of that journey towards what can be done. I think that platforms like Wikipedia are proof that vast populations can craft accurate and complex documents, so maybe it is in fact possible to bypass the creation of a constitutional council in the way that Iceland did. My perspective in this situation is that it is useful to create a starting point until there is sufficient documentation and sufficient quality to allow bigger groups (e.g. everybody in a country) to edit and iterate on something.

This is in fact the reason I decided to author this book myself as a starting point rather than crowdsourcing it from the start (which I considered). I am confident that once a good starting point is created we can hand over total ownership of this body of knowledge to everybody.

My hypothesis is that once we have a constitutional starting point as shown in Iceland's example, we could then hand this over to something like a wiki for people to constantly update and edit, that way the constitution will constantly evolve. This could get confusing of course because if the rules are changing everyday, how do we know what behaviour lies inside and outside of the rules? I think from a practical perspective it could be feasible to have timeframes and cut off points.

For instance, we could edit the constitution until 31st Dec and whatever is in there at the cut off time is applicable for the next 3 months. During those 3 months we keep editing for the following 3 months...etc. This is a simplistic idea, the details would of course have to be ironed out and would no doubt be more complex but I think the tech is there to have a genuinely always evolving governance system. Ultimately, the mechanism itself would also be something for the people to decide on.

So who knows, maybe it will be possible to bypass this representative element of democracy as we develop our knowledge and experience in crowdsourcing qualitative information.

What can a crowd do and what can't it do?

Is it possible to ask large groups to craft something that is so nuanced and subtle as a constitution? Voting is often a simple binary process, so it isn't too difficult to assume that we will be doing that from technological platforms very quickly (we already are in some instances).

For qualitative data however, is this possible? Again, as above, I think so. It's clearly been possible for complex networked products like Wikipedia and Linux, so why not for other things like a constitution? Again, we are relatively immature in our application of this right now, but it's definitely not stupid to assume that once this constitution finally passes, it may be iterated on constantly in a wiki-like platform.

What is the role of intermediaries or representatives if any?

This is something that I think the Icelandic Constitution highlights beautifully. The council of 25 people were elected, and once elected they were facilitators of a process. Their own opinion of course will have been in there, but it was secondary to the request for citizen participation and to their role in summarising the will of an entire nation. This mirrors Adam's (MiVote) intention for the role of representative to move from an empire-building career to a temporary civic duty, something like what many countries have for jury duty.

Every week on a Friday the Icelandic Constitutional Council put their work online, seeking feedback and input from the country, including their thoughts and comments as they went along, constantly improving. In the initial phase each of the 100 tables of 10 citizens had a facilitator to help them articulate their thoughts and beliefs. If this is anything to go by, a big part of the skills needed by representatives (if we are to have any of course) will be the facilitation to harvest the people's will. This feels ethically truer and more effective in creating representative outcomes from a population's beliefs.

To me, this project shows how far politics has strayed from representing the people and shows that any government of the future needs a new set of skills. One with a richer, more enlightened understanding of integral theory (see Ken Wilbur on this attempt *"to draw together an already existing number of separate paradigms into an interrelated network of approaches that are mutually enriching"*) and with the nuance and skills necessary to create a sense of alignment amongst citizens.

Back to Finnur. Now let's talk about this small group in more detail. How did the constitutional council of 30 people look and work?

We had an election where anyone could run. It was quite unique as well. It was an individual election and a lot of people ran, so a lot of people were interested in taking part in the council and we had hundreds of people that ran, but we had 30 members elected. They didn't anticipate so many participants when they passed the election, so they had to come up with a way to create the polls and how we were going to sort this out, so they used the single transferable vote method, which has been used in Ireland and other places - people create a sorted list, they can choose as many people on the ballot and put them in an order.

This is then calculated and you get a result, and the result was actually a very nice cross-section of the nation. You had a priest, a lawyer, a couple of mathematicians, you had the board member of a big games company. Of course there was some bias towards some people who had been writing articles in the news...etc. It had a disabled person in a wheelchair, young representatives. It was a good mix, and it didn't seem to be influenced a lot by political parties, as such. It was just quite a random sample that was elected.

The group was really motivated to do a good job so we sat down and decided - "ok, we've got 6 months to write a constitution", and they were in the mindset to create a full new document. So we got in agile coaches from CCP which is a big online multiplayer games producer in Iceland, and the constitution council created like a tourist guide for Iceland in three iterations during a day - just to get acquainted with agile methodology.

This was one of the hard moments in the process, so we decided to adapt weekly sprints - we would work in groups, and every Friday, we would take the results of our work, publish it, and then repeat. So rather than spending 6 months on writing one document and then putting it to the people, we would just publish the progress every week.

So they did this for months until they ended up with a final constitution. This was then voted in by 70% of the people. There is a final twist in the story, but before we go there, I'd like to summarise the process that we've heard from Finnur. Diagrammatically, it could look something like this:

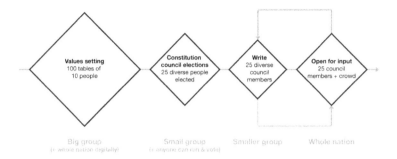

There is something in the detail of this process, which I
think is perhaps the most important thing of all. This
process wasn't about deciding on the 'What' (on policy),
or on the 'Who' (on parties), it was about deciding on the
'Where to' and the 'How'. It was about deciding what kind
of country we want to be in the future and what principles
we need to get there. It was about deciding what kind of
world we want our children to grow up in. In Finnur's
words:

*The main thing for me is that if, or when, we finally
get this constitution passed, I know a few people
that we can track through the comments. Some
people could say to their grandchildren, "you see
this article here in the constitution, I influenced
that." I took part in writing the reactions to the
clause about the internet and I have a few words in
there, so if it gets passed as the constitution, I
could tell my daughter that "your father actually*

wrote these words in the constitution bill." That is quite powerful, if we actually manage to get this one approved, we would have had input from people that actually shaped the document. It wasn't just a group of individuals selected by the parliament to do this thing, it actually came from wide audiences. Thousands of people participated in making a document, many of them can actually point to it and say "I helped write this."

And so it is through conversations in an auditorium, on social media, in forums, in debate, in the council, that the country of Iceland decided on its destination. A destination which upholds the values of:

- Equality
- Democracy
- Honesty
- Human-rights
- Justice
- Respect
- Freedom

So what came of this constitution? Let's ask Finnur again:

I need to explain some of the complications, because not everyone was happy with this work.

There were a couple of people that challenged the election based on technicalities, because the ballot was quite big. It was a big A3 paper because you had to fit all of the people on there. Then you had to slide it into a ballot box.

Someone said, based on Icelandic election laws, if someone sees what you're voting, it's illegal. So they took it to the high court and said the election wasn't legal. No-one actually said that anyone had seen anyone else's vote, and no-one was challenging the result of the election, but the high court actually decided to deem the election void. There's lots of conspiracy theories and everything else around it.

Me, utterly staggered: *"Just because the ballot was on an A3 sheet of paper?!"*

Yes, someone could've seen your ballot. There has been a lot of writing about this. The idea is that there is a power struggle in Iceland about who controls the country. Is it the people who control the money? Or the fish? Or whatever? And this is the only example of such a ruling, but this was maybe designed specifically to trip up the process.

And so if there is any example of why we should let the people rule over professional politicians, businesses and lobbyists it is this. Despite 70% of a nation deciding on the future of that nation, the powerful minority can still pull out a trump card which is so transparently against the will of the people.

But not to worry, there is still hope. The Icelandic Pirate Party is gaining in power and they aim to push the formal acceptance of this constitution and implement it as the new official constitution of Iceland. Never has that famous Steve Jobs quote been more appropriate: *"I'd rather be a pirate than join the navy."*

In conclusion

I find the story of the Icelandic Crowdsourced Constitution beyond inspiring. For such an epic thing to come from a grassroots movement with a name like 'The Ministry of Ideas' is unbelievable. It is believed by many to be a key milestone to the future of our democracies. When addressing a debate on the future of this constitution in Iceland, the globally respected Harvard Law Professor Lawrence Lessig said the following:

> *Here's the question: What are you going to do for democracy in the world?*

That sounds like an odd question to ask in Iceland, it's a small place, you might not think of yourselves as central to the future of democracy in the world. But I want to do in the next three minutes is convince you just why Iceland is so central to the future of democracy in the world.

Because if you think about democracy across the world, it's failing across the world. And it's failing because ordinary people feel like their leaders, don't listen to them. And like a five year old child at a certain point, they have to act out. And they have to act out in a way that gets the attention of their leaders. So think about what's happened in Britain with Brexit and Germany with the AFD Party, or in the United States with Donald Trump.

I am a democrat. And I believe it is critical to show people around the world that democracy is actually possible. That people can actually do something. And that's why I came here to Iceland with my family this fall. Because 8 years ago when you, like the rest of the world, when you confronted the collapse of your economy, you discovered that that collapse was tied to a problem in your government. And what you did in response to that was something nobody else in the world did. You motivated each other to begin a process of constitutional reform, a crowdsourced constitution.

And after that process you had an election, a referendum, where more than 2/3rds of Icelanders endorsed the idea of the constitution. And when I tell this story around the world about each of these chapters, people are amazed. Then I tell the story that the parliament did not adopt the constitution, and they are amazed again. Because they can't understand how such an extraordinary expression of democratic will is ignored.

If the next chapter of this story were that the opposition parties here agreed to make this change fundamental, then that too would be an extraordinary, surprising next step in the story of how democracy in Iceland had worked.

Now, I think you need a constitution but I don't really argue for this because of what you need. I think we, citizens of the world, need an example of democracy working. And the reason we need you to do this, is I'm sure it will make your democracy work better, but it will make the possibility of democracy around the world seem hopeful again. And we can take this story all around the world and say 'we can learn and follow the lead that happened that happens here'.

You started something extraordinary 6 years ago and that chapter, the next chapter, can make that story even more extraordinary. So I'm grateful we're having this conversation and I'm eager to hear what we can do to make this hopefulness for democracy something the whole world can celebrate. Thank you.

In summary, here is what I think are the main takeaways of such an open and inspiring process:

Citizen centricity: They not only asked and listened to citizens, they asked ordinary citizens to actually lead the process.

Deliberative democracy: The new constitution was deliberated in open online forums to build a better result for everybody.

Representatives as facilitators: The role of citizen was so active and was actually that of a politician, one whose job it is to integrate different perspectives.

Qualitative constitutional approach: They managed to involve people on mass scale in such a nuanced process where the importance of language and subtlety is so high.

I hope only that this constitution quickly becomes official and real as it deserves to be. An example for politicians around the world to follow.

pol.is
& vTaiwan

Key principles
Qualitative coherence at scale
Machine learning
Involving citizens upstream
Designed for nuance and conversation

*The technology enabled a process of lawmaking that
allowed for greater scale and better quality of input earlier
in the lawmaking process in Taiwan, and broke deadlocks
among stakeholders along the way.*

Colin Megill

Why is this interesting?

We need to pull away from the binary and partisan ideological approach of party politics, and embrace the nuance of what it is to hold multiple perspectives at any given time. Holding and integrating multiple viewpoints on the world is pretty fundamental to human evolution. For example, if I ask you: 'is abortion good or bad?' You will probably have a gut reaction either way.

Upon inspection and debate most people will probably find that their perspective varies dependent on the context. In some situations I am 'pro-life' and in other instances I might be 'pro-choice' as per the complexity of such a nuanced issue. In binary politics, you have to vote for a party which will hold a clear stance on that, but may be against other policies you believe in. Under our current systems you have to buy them wholesale. Red or Blue? No room for nuance.

With tools like pol.is, this nuance is the very foundation of the conversation and building future modes of governance around conversation is surely something we should aspire to. Conversation about the societies we want to create and for those conversations to lead to tangible outcomes as in the example of the passing of new Uber legislation with vTaiwan.

Pre-internet there were clear reasons why it was difficult to have a fully decentralised governance process, or to implement true direct democracy: the technology just wasn't there. It was for obvious reasons, impossible for everybody to make decisions on everything all the time. The manpower needed for such a democratic system would have been astronomical. The result of this is that most countries now have a centralised system based on a range of political ideologies that lie somewhere along the left-right political spectrum. However, the ideologies of specific parties are not necessarily 'representative' of the people's view. These ideologies lack the nuance and granularity of the way the world is really viewed by a diverse population.

In the digital age, decision-making and mass communication is much simpler, but until recently, still not simple enough for true direct democracy. To decentralise all decision making at this point could create more noise and chaos. We are still a long way from figuring out what to do with all the big and small data that we are creating. IBM estimates that:

> *Every day, we create 2.5 quintillion bytes of data — so much that 90% of the data in the world today has been created in the last two years alone. This data comes from everywhere: sensors used to*

gather climate information, posts to social media sites, digital pictures and videos, purchase transaction records, and cell phone GPS signals to name a few. This data is big data.

For our political process to be opened up in this digital environment is a worrying prospect for many.

This was before machine learning and artificial intelligence matured to the stages they have done recently. In the last couple of years, a lot has happened. Google's 'Deep Mind' beat the World Champion of 'Go'. A piece of software figured out our 150 year dilemma as to why worms that are cut in half create two worms, making it the first time a scientific finding is attributed to a computer rather than a human. And in the commercial arena, Google, Apple and Amazon are all racing to create the most sophisticated AI assistants they can.

What this means is machine learning and AI are reaching stages where they can understand many-to-many conversations in a way that human beings cannot. We now have the technology to cope with exponentiality and to decentralise decision making without chaos ensuing. We can decentralise decision making and create mass participation, all with a system built to create coherent conversations at scale. Think of it like this:

*Pace of change + centralised government =
breaking system*

Pace of change + decentralisation = chaotic system

*Pace of change + (decentralistion + AI) = mass
coherence*

This is why 'pol.is', and particularly its application in Taiwan is interesting. Because machine learning is now being used for large numbers of people to shape public policy in a way that allows for nuance and granularity. In this chapter we look into pol.is and the vTaiwan story and hear more about the work they are doing. To give you an overview, this is how pol.is describe their mission & vision on their website:

pol.is was conceived around the time of Occupy Wall Street and the Arab Spring. We felt if millions of people were going to show up to a conversation, the internet needed something that would scale up. We set out to build a communication system that would handle 'big' and stay coherent. We wanted people to feel safe & listened to, and we felt it was of the highest importance that minority opinions be preserved rather than 'outvoted'.

Most generally, we leverage advances in mobile connectivity, artificial intelligence and machine learning to build tools that provide transparency, produce insight and decentralize power in all kinds of organizations of people everywhere on Earth.

Pol.is Mission & Vision

Before we hear from the people behind pol.is and vTaiwan, here are four main reasons why I think this is exciting…

Qualitative coherence at scale: This feels like an evolution of the language processing and summarising process used in the Icelandic Crowdsourced Constitution. By using machine learning, the pol.is team have managed to create a platform which can make big scale conversations constructive and coherent, resulting in tangible outputs.

Machine learning: Right now there are basically two technologies that everybody is talking about: blockchain and machine learning. The application of this relatively nascent technology to the world of civic tech and govtech is an example of early adoption applied to a sector which is notoriously lagging when it comes to technology.

Involving citizens upstream: In modern democracies, citizens rarely get a say in the shaping of policies. Governments tend to do this work without involving citizens in this part of the process. The impact of any feedback tends to be small because it comes late in the process. If governments are willing to deploy it, the pol.is platform facilitates citizen participation from the very beginning. We can only 'enact the will of the people' if we first ask what that will is.

Designed for nuance and conversation: Systems of governance which only involve the electorate in up/down votes are letting us all down, no matter which side you're on. pol.is enables discussions with large groups with all of the nuance that those conversations demand. This results in tangible decisions and policy changes which are truly representative of the will of the people, as they have emerged directly from the people.

pol.is & vTaiwan
in their own words

Before explaining how pol.is works and how they see the
world, I'd like to start by sharing the story of how the
technology was applied in real life, in Taiwan. I've
compiled their amazing story from Wikipedia articles,
chats with pol.is, and from blog posts by civichall.org's Liz
Barry.

You may find the Iceland story amazing and inspiring but
some cynics have immediately responded saying things
like 'you would expect that from Iceland, their a small,
rich, scandinavian country. This wouldn't work in other
cultures.'

Not true. One of the best examples of mass civic
participation using technology comes from Taiwan, which
has a population of 25million people. The context for this
is Taiwan's Sunflower Demonstration, a student-led
movement in opposition to the government's new trade
deal with Beijing that turned into a weeks-long occupation
of the country's parliament. The protesters asked for a
rejection of the trade agreement, the passing of legislation

allowing close monitoring of future agreements with China, and citizen conferences discussing constitutional amendment.

As this movement sustained and developed, technology became an increasingly important part of the process and turned into a project called vTaiwan. According to Liz Barry from civichall.org:

> *The process now routinely leads to passages of laws by Taiwan's national legislature. And it's gaining momentum: on July 26, Taiwan's new premier declared in a cross-ministry meeting that "all substantial national issues should go through a vTaiwan-like process."*

Like Iceland, vTaiwan uses technology, media, and facilitation to help develop constructive conversations amongst citizens. vTaiwan is now working on scaling facilitation skills as a critical component of the democratic process.

They also use the pol.is technology, followed by a broadcasted public meeting where scholars and officials respond to issues that emerged in the conversation. An in-person stakeholder meeting co-facilitated by civil society and the government is then broadcast to remote participants before the Government agrees to take action related to areas that reached consensus, or provides a point-by-point explanation of why those consensus points aren't feasible. Liz Barry goes on to explain:

> *Once vTaiwan deployed pol.is, participation scaled a hundredfold, the complexity of issues grappled with increased, and the volunteer moderators were no longer needed during the "crowd-sourced agenda setting" phase. After years of closely iterating with the vTaiwan team, pol.is was recently open sourced, greenlighting its longterm integration into governing processes.*

pol.is is an impressive piece of technology in its ability to create clarity from large scale qualitative conversations. Their co-founder Colin Megill describes the platform's impact in Taiwan:

> *The technology enabled a process of lawmaking that allowed for greater scale and better quality of input earlier in the lawmaking process in Taiwan, and broke deadlocks among stakeholders along the way.*

To understand the details of pol.is and its application in the vTaiwan process better, let's look at a specific example where the country was debating how to approach the growth of Uber. This democratic process led to legislation change specifically around safety, as was the will of the people. The results were outlined as follows by Taiwan's Digital Minister Audrey Tang on the pol.is blog:

On May 23, 2016, the Administration pledged to ratify all the pol.is consensus items into a new regulation:
- *Taxis no longer need to be painted yellow.*
- *High-end app-based Taxis are free to operate, as long as they don't undercut existing meters.*
- *App-based dispatch systems must display car and driver identification, estimated fare, and customer rating.*
- *Per-ride taxation is required to report to the Ministry of Finance.*

With this regulation, other Uber-like apps, some created by the civil society, are entering the market.

This is the result of a use of artificial intelligence to really listen to the people and to pair that with in-person meetings (transcribed and published for transparency) with experts, in order to come to good, educated and fast conclusions.

The process was designed
- **collaboratively**, with participants crowd-sourcing meeting agendas via 4 weeks of public survey on pol.is, complete with Uber's own analysis on the raw data.
- **transparently**, with 1,875 online participants joining the two-hour live-streamed meeting with academics, industry experts, and representatives from Association of Taxi Drivers in Taipei, Taiwan Taxi, Uber, The Ministries of Transport, Economic Affairs, and Finance.

It has resulted not just in legislation changes but also in better relationships and possible partnerships between previously competitive organisations.

This story gives me hope for several reasons. It shows that genuine direct democracy is possible. It shows that good quality conversations can scale and be coherent thanks to technology. It shows that these processes lead to real tangible benefits and the numbers show that people want to be involved in these processes.

I think it is also an example of how digital democratic processes are possible in diverse cultures across the world. The internet can be the platform upon which the future of governance and civil participation is built. We've now heard from Australia, Iceland. We will soon hear from Argentina and Estonia, and we just heard from Taiwan. A testament to this growing movement. All made possible thanks to modern tech.

Having learnt about the success of pol.is in Taiwan, I asked Colin to tell me more about the technology, where the story started and where it's led them:

> *I started thinking about this problem around when I was 20 years old or so, I'm 31 now. At that time I was in college, studying international relations and political science. A very big picture question at the time was 'why do humans still have difficulty coordinating in groups?' That's a very fundamental thing, and it's led to businesses often quickly moving away from democracy and towards dictatorship as they scale. We scale out of coordinating our behavior very quickly. Forget going to millions of people, we just have representatives. How do you scale up people's ability to coordinate their behavior? What are the blockages to that?*

This scaling problem is spot on to me. It is one of the

reasons why centralisation, rigid hierarchy and autocracy are such default modes. As discussed, in the past we haven't have the technology to decentralise human behaviour. Coordinating coherance was the challenge that faced technological limitations in the past, and it is the challenge that Colin and pol.is took on:

> *Fast forward. I'm still thinking about this. Occupy Wall Street happens and Tahrir Square happens. Twitter plays a big part in that. Twitter is really good for mobilization. So we have mobilization, but it's mobilization without things like aggregating common opinions and synthesizing them, getting these people to talk together in the same space, there's a lot of energy going into the system without any order after that. What do we need in terms of order after we get people out into the streets? You can't write a constitution on Twitter. That's one of the things that I was thinking about early on.*

Social media's role in the Arab Spring, and other social movements like Occupy Wall Street, shows the potential the web has for mobilisation. So far, this has mainly been done in unofficial networks, after all, revolutions tend to happen outside of official forums. There is one example from inside a system which has shown great potential.

The UK's Government Digital Service (GDS) created an e-petition platform (in an impressive 8 weeks) on which citizens can write a petition to parliament. If any petition gets 10,000 signatures, they receive a response from the government. If they get 100,000 signatures the issue will be a subject of debate in the British parliament. This has led to the consideration of topics from free Meningitis B vaccines, immigration, anti-war campaigns, EU involvement, and many many more. It's a great start.

I'm not sure if there will be politicians in the future, or if there should be. This discussion around mobilisation however does show a future form of leadership, one where a social movement can start, spread and gain legitimacy, particularly when combined with direct forms of democracy as we saw with MiVote. Somebody could start a movement, a petition could gain traction, a robust and thorough direct democracy process could ensue in response to this petition. Government by the people for the people. End to end. Colin explained the development of pol.is further:

> It was very elementary in the way that I had conceived it. I moved to Seattle and connected with two co-founders, Michael Bjorkegren and Christopher Small. Over the next year or so we kind of workshopped this problem with their

background from AI and statistical analysis, and our collective passion for data visualization, and felt like, "Okay, what could we do to produce a new technology that would enable new possibilities?"

We were trying to basically solve the problem from a perspective of, how do you scale this up? That's core to everything we've been doing. How do you scale to 100,000 people communicating effectively together with something?

This is a hard problem, and the growth of machine learning and artificial intelligence will be paramount to this evolution. pol.is and its application in vTaiwan that we saw above demonstrates the sizeable benefits that AI can bring for citizens to move from mobilisation to mass coherence. This is starting to enable large numbers of people to be part of conversations early on in the process in a way that produces concrete and beneficial results.

I recommend you play with the pol.is website to see just how simple and easy this can be. Of course, there is complexity here, but that is given in our complex world. This process created coherence (defined by Audrey Tang as 'rough consensus') amongst a huge group of people, in order to eventually change laws at a faster rate and more effectively than is traditionally the case in centralised governance structures.

In conclusion

To me this is an incredible advance in our ability to listen to citizens, and to create the coherence necessary to do something about it. If politics exists to 'enact the will of the people', it must first know what the people's will is in the first place! Tools like pol.is make that possible all the time, en masse and it is only getting better and better. In 2016, there is no excuse for not asking the people what they want by having many-to-many conversations, to not do so is by definition undemocratic.

I have learnt a lot from this story. A new angle, a tangible tool and a new piece to the puzzle that this book is exploring. These are my take outs from Colin's work at pol.is and the vTaiwan case study.

> **Qualitative coherence at scale:** It's possible to not only mobilise people around topics, but also to create coherence (not consensus) around these conversations

> **Machine learning:** This technology is getting smarter by the day and could be the solution to creating this coherence at scale

Involving citizens upstream: Citizens can be made a part of the decision from the very beginning. Not just as a gesture once everything is done.

Designed for nuance and conversation: True conversation around topics, can lead to detailed decisions which are right for the people not for the parties.

Democracy Earth & DemocracyOS

Key principles
Digital direct democracy
Change from inside the system
Informal governmental accountability

I'm all in for the idea of turning the internet into a planetary jurisdiction that can operate anywhere in the world and really address the challenges of the 21st century.

- Santiago Siri

Democracy Earth & DemocracyOS in a nutshell

When a group of young Argentinian techies with revolutionary tendencies felt disenfranchised at the old and outdated political system, they decided to do something about it. They created a sort of dummy political party called the 'Net Party' as an offline extension of a revolutionary online platform they named 'DemocracyOS'.

DemocracyOS is kind of a big deal inside tech/democracy circles and after getting funding from one of Silicon Valley's most respected investment companies, the seed accelerator YCombinator, it now has even bigger ambitions which it calls 'Democracy Earth'. They aim to use blockchain technology and an open source philosophy to revolutionise politics by creating a digital direct democracy platform.

Because direct democracy isn't legitimate within the existing Argentine political system, DemocracyOS wasn't legitimate either. Which is why, whilst DemocracyOS allowed any citizen to vote on direct policies using a smartphone app, they also created a party which would enact the results of those votes, or at least show the dissonance between the expressed will of the people and the reality of political decision making.

Why is this interesting?

Digital direct democracy: we've discussed how technology makes the notion of true direct democracy possible and Democracy Earth makes this idea super tangible. Voting directly on policy is possible through a simple voting mechanism. Is there any need for politicians anymore?!

Change from inside the system: Unfortunately, the current system isn't ready for this, so the only way to make the people's decisions count for something was to create a dummy party inside the parliament that could follow the requests of citizens. An interesting and innovative way to work within the constraints of an existing system.

Informal governmental accountability: If changing the system from the inside still doesn't get big enough results, putting politicians under pressure is made possible by making the electorate's expressed needs publicly visible. This mean any subsequent discord between what people want and what politicians do is also visible.

Democracy Earth & DemocracyOS in their own words

Having heard about the 'Where to' from MiVote and about the 'How' from Finnur and Iceland's Crowdsourced Constitution, we will now get into the 'What' by speaking to the inspiring Santiago Siri, Democracy Earth's co-founder and practical philosopher.

Here's the story...

Dismayed by a political system that hasn't changed for hundreds of years, Argentinian political scientists Pia Mancini & Santiago Siri wanted to explore new solutions for the internet era. Their answer was to found the 'Net Party' and 'DemocracyOS', an open source web application designed to build a bridge between citizens and elected representatives. The aim is to enable a more direct form of democracy by allowing citizens to vote on real policies and to influence politicians' decisions by showing them the data illustrative of the population's perspectives.

This free software allows citizens to get informed, debate

and vote on every single bill presented in Congress. It is available in 15 languages and according to the Democracy OS website:

> *It has been used in Tunisia to debate its national constitution; by the Federal Government of Mexico to develops its open government policy; by the youngest parliamentarian in Kenya to consult his constituency and by the Congress of Buenos Aires becoming the first experience on digital democracy in the American continent.*

The backstory of a political millennial

I spoke to Santiago Siri, co-founder of the NetParty, DemocracyOS and Democracy Earth to find out more. Here's a little bit about him:

> *The bottom line with me is that I started programming computers at a very young age, when I was 9-10 and early on, my passion was to develop video games. I am 33 years old now and I started my career as a game developer. I did whatever I could to get to San Francisco and learn from the best game developers here in this town and take it from there.*

While making games, I realised that I always cared for games that have some social impact in any way and later on in my career I found myself trying to make what are called 'serious games' or games that mean either to express a political message or for training purposes. Eventually I started developing web software - technology for the web, and the deeper I dived into that, the more I realised that after all, the internet is certainly changing every aspect of our lives and eventually, that initial dream of doing games that have some social impact turns out that actual reality is in some way or another a kind of game.

The financial reality is a score ranking game, the political reality is a theatrical play and it's just a matter of time before the games that we play will eventually shape the institutions we create.

The last 4-5 years, I found myself doing politics. The reason I did that jump to politics was a wake up call I had when I was invited as an entrepreneur and I was coming from the tech sector in Argentina, I was invited to the World Economic Forum and I met a lot of like-minded people from my generation that were my age back then - 25/26 years old. I remember meeting this Chilean guy, Giorgio

Jackson, who was the leader of the student movement in Chilé, an activist, he led 3 million people to the streets in Chilé to reform the education laws in his country.

When I met him I realised that instead of talking with a traditional politician I was talking with a millennial - someone from my generation - we were talking about memes, we were talking about social media, about Twitter. I realised that that was the way our whole generation actually looks at everything, not just digital stuff, but everything, even politics.

Learning from a guy like him who was my age, and suddenly realising that when the turn of our generation comes, the one thing we have that is totally different from previous generations is definitely the internet. We're called millennials, but in our adolescence, it's really the internet that shaped our minds, rather than the year 2000.

There I decided to make the jump towards starting up something in politics in Argentina, which is a very troubling country and has a lot of issues. I lived there for 30 years and it has been systematic *confrontation and fraud and corruption across throughout all our young democracy, and there's where I decided to startup a political party like the NetParty and figure out if my entrepreneurial technology knowledge could contribute in any possible way. The last five years have been quite challenging to say the least.*

My first attempt at politics - as a teenager I was very idealistic and I read a couple of biographies of Ché Guevara and I suddenly had the 'red fever' at home, and I put up the posters... my teen idol was Ché Guevarra... I was 18/19 years old, I was very young and my father said, "You like this guy? Go to Cuba" *and he invited me to go to Cuba for one month and see how the Cuban revolution was actually going on over there, and I spent - in Cuba - one full month, living in the house of former revolutionaries that fought along with Ché Guevara and I remember that in one of the homes, there was this teenager, my age as well and he had a little dog and I asked him the name of his dog and he says* "the name of my dog is Linux." *There was this kid, also my generation, in Cuba, whose dream was to get connected, to be online. All he could have*

was a computer with Windows, sometimes he
would get some kind of access and he had a little
dog whose name was Linux.

That was my first heartbreak with politics because I
realised that I was trapped in a 1984 Orwellian
nightmare - at least, that's what Cuba really is, Fidel
Castro on TV every day and there's where my
dream for pursuing anything political stopped and I
decided to take an entrepreneurial road and focus
on building technology. 7-8 years later, I met
Giorgio Jackson and that spark reignited again and
I got back to my political calling. But always with a
clear idea that if it's to try the same ideas that have
been tried before, it's not worth it.

Don't get me wrong, a year later, after I was in
Cuba I was trading stocks on Wall Street so maybe
there I was a little bit too far on the other side, but I
tend to think now that I'm more stable. The best
things happen when you cross-pollinate mindsets
and merging technology and politics is a whole new
world. It really hasn't been tried until recently with
the rise of the Pirate Party and all these new things
that are happening all over the world right now.
That speaks about a new generation - political
change happens at glacial speeds, it's very slow,

but it has to do with one generation dying and one generation growing up, and technology is moving at an accelerated speed, so it's an interesting collision of worlds.

Hacking politics with a Trojan Horse strategy

One thing that really drew me to Santi's story is the approach he used to work within the context of this slow change in politics, and as he says, the dying of one generation and the maturation of another. Since writing this, I've heard a lot of *"it's not possible to change the existing system"* kind of talk. Which, whilst I understand, I just don't think is a useful perspective. What Santi and his colleagues did was take a new approach to this. Rather than fighting from the outside only, they used what he describes as a 'Trojan Horse' tactic:

> *In 2012. A little bit over four years ago. In April 2012 (we started) with the very simple idea of trying to hack politics with a Trojan Horse tactic, where we have a party that has candidates committed to always vote according to what citizens decide online. We had to figure out how to do that party, how to run for elections and discover how incredibly nasty and corrupt the political system*

actually is, and on the other hand, develop the right kind of technology so we can get on board as many citizens as we can to participate.

We started in 2012 with a group of friends and colleagues coming from the technological scene. One of these friends - his wife used to be a legislator in the city of Buenos Aires, and I remember pitching her this idea of, "what happens if we go to the city congress and try to create a candidate that will always vote according to the internet?" *And I remember that she said,* "I'm not sure this is going to work, but I'm definitely positive that it's much better than anything else that we have in congress right now."

This to me, is quite an amazing and almost satirical image of just how removed politics can be, not only from people but from technology too. This idea of a dummy party with dummy politicians, who go along with whatever society wants, is so simple and yet so progressive an approach to help change the way we are governed.

That was our first validation to the idea and from there onwards, we started talking with a lot of like-minded friends and some of them joined us.

Starting up a political party is really a collective effort because there will be no money in it - money is always only on the big parties, there will be no other thing other than citizens willing to bring some idealistic change to their city, to their community. We started doing meetings every friday night, the meetings were codenamed 'Alcohol, Narcotics, Politics and Technology', and we started talking late at night about what it would take to make a political party of this kind, and we kept on inviting friends, it kept snowballing and we had a very clear objective because we started in 2012, and we realised that the elections were happening in October 2013.

We had that target of the elections of October 2013 and that aligned every incentive of the group that we were to prepare ourselves to be able to run for the election. We figured out what was required, we collected the signatures, we developed the branding, we started inviting more friends and as the election day approached, it was really quite incredible because a lot of people joined us and we were able to run for elections and we got 1.2% of the vote.

We were a very disruptive offering in the very

*traditional spectrum of Argentina and it was a good
start for us. At the same time, I started developing
the technology, which is an open source software,
so we can figure out the way to get people
engaged and willing to participate using this open
source software to debate the bills that are in
congress, or the ideas that are from the party.*

A foot in the new world and a foot in the old world

*The first MVP that we developed is called
DemocracyOS and it was a very simple piece of
technology. It's an open source project - it has
contributors now from all over the world, it's a
Javascript application written in Node and Mongo
DB. The way it works is: you get informed, you
debate, and you vote on bills. That's it. It's
extremely straightforward, very simple, adaptive to
any screen. It was the minimum viable product we
needed.*

Remember MiVote's 6 step process? Well, this is where it
started, in Argentina, with Santi and a simple 3 step
process to involve citizens in defining their destiny. The
platform now allows people to not only vote (yay, nay or
abstain) but also to deliberate the policies themselves in

forums attached to each topic. People can also raise their own topics in order to start discussion around areas they believe are particularly important.

The simple effectiveness of being open source

The main reason it got traction, it got useage, I think it's definitely because it was an open source project. A lot of folks in the civic activist communities from all round the world liked it it because of that and they decided to adapt it to use it in different ways. While we were doing the party, suddenly the software took off and it was being used in Tunisia to update the national constitution, by a political party in Spain, by some cities near São Paulo in Brazil, it was localised into many languages and a community was built around it, and the software, as an open source project, because it was relatively well known in the space of civic technology.

Social movements have always grown organically as they spread across nations, but the internet obviously amplifies the potential for this greatly. Open source is a pretty common thing, but I can't help think that the mixture of Santi's revolutionary and philosophical tendencies, matched with his technical abilities are almost symbolic of a generation (my generation) which is creating change in new ways at a scale and speed we've never seen before. To refer back to some of the distributed and anti-fragile notions we discussed earlier in this book, technology means that in some ways a movement like this can't be quashed. Once the fire is lit, it can spread easily, with activists in different countries adding fuel to it when needed to support their own causes.

Growing up and increasing the impact

After the election of 2013, we focused more on the development of the software, and in 2014, we got a call from YCombinator (probably the most important investment firm in Silicon valley) *and they decided to back us as a non-profit. So that's what brought me to California. Here, we started focusing more on the technology, we built the Democracy Earth foundation, that's what I'm running right now, and with all the lessons that we learnt with the NetParty and DemocracyOS, we're now working on a much more robust and interesting technology.*

Learning from failure

The most important thing about all of this is also the flaws that we discovered. There were many. When interests are high, systems will get hacked, politics will get manipulated and we also had our wake-up call in that respect.

As I read this little paragraph, from a transatlantic flight, I'm reminded of the book about failure in the airline industry and how it is approached. In *'Black Box Thinking'*, Matthew Syed outlines the cognitive bias and cognitive dissonance that we all experience. Moments where all the information we see seems to confirm the view of reality we've constructed, thus creating a 'closed loop' approach to learning which basically means you can't learn anymore.

'Black Box Thinking' shows how devastating this has been in the healthcare industry leading to 100,000s medical errors sometimes with fatal consequences. Taleb quotes figures of between 44,000 and 98,000 Americans dying each year as a result of preventable medical errors, making it the third biggest killer in the United States.

The book goes on to quote health research scholar Nancy Berlinger:

Observing more senior physicians, students learn that their mentors and supervisors believe in, practice and reward the concealment of errors. They learn how to talk about unanticipated outcomes until a "mistake" morphs into a "complication". Above all, they learn not to tell the patient anything.

Syed isn't trying to pick on healthcare professionals though, he even gives example of his own tendency for dissonant thinking. But his most extreme example comes from politics and the words of Tony Blair and George W. Bush in the aftermath of the Iraq War. He shows that for each time their mistakes (regarding weapons of mass destruction existing) were picked up, they seemed to grow stronger in their convictions, distorting facts and creating different memories or rhetoric for events. Again, he's not actually saying they even did this intentionally, just that is an observable and commonplace phenomenon.

Here with Santi, we see the 'learning from failure' gospel that pervades the world of tech entrepreneurship is deeply needed in politics. It is one which constantly changes and iterates, improving the user experience systematically. In this case it is improving the citizen experience systematically. Santi's Democracy OS is another example of user centricity in these pioneering case studies, and not the last. The need for agility in politics has never been clearer. Anyway, back to Santi…

Cloud vs Land: eroding borders and the future of planetary jurisdiction

I learned a lot about how corrupt the political system is in Argentina - many more stories to share about that - and also from the technology point of view, we discovered many of the flaws and the challenges that are required.

The most interesting thing going on in the world right now, in my view, coming from this technology-meets-politics mindset, is certainly the rise of blockchain-based technology. The importance of blockchains is that ultimately it's a bureaucracy. Simply put, it is able to verify events in a way that removes the notion of lack of trust from the equation. Ultimately, nation states are bureaucracies, cities are bureaucracies. So the interesting element looking forward is… we are in a context right now that is really more and more starting to look like the cloud versus the land.

In the land - rising nationalism, industrial mindset,

*trying to control our bodies. In the cloud -
corporations owning our data and privacy, and
trying to control our information, our attention. In
this cloud versus the land, the whole thesis around
decentralisation and blockchain-based technology
speaks about the possibility of creating a grid
where we can localise computing and empower
people around the world in completely new ways.*

*The main quest looking forward is, can we really
turn the internet into a planetary jurisdiction? Can
we really erode the borders of nation states? And I
think that the more we dive into this cloud versus
land context, the more relevant the internet
becomes. Especially as we face planetary issues
that cannot be addressed simply by national
structures.*

That's right. He said *"turn the internet into a planetary
jurisdiction"*.

I remember this point so clearly when speaking to Santi.
Goosebumps. I'm repeatedly inspired by the activists,
applying powerful and accessible technology to the
rigorous critical and visionary thinking they have
developed. This particular part reminded me of an
expression coined by Thomas L. Friedman in the New

York Times. He talks about a new political struggle not between left and right, or democrats and republicans, but between *"Wall People" and "Web People."* Friedman goes on to say:

Web People instinctively understand that Democrats and Republicans both built their platforms largely in response to the Industrial Revolution, the New Deal and the Cold War, but that today, a 21st-century party needs to build its platform in response to the accelerations in technology, globalization and climate change, which are the forces transforming the workplace, geopolitics and the very planet.

As such, the instinct of Web People is to embrace the change in the pace of change and focus on empowering more people to be able to compete and collaborate in a world without walls. In particular, Web People understand that in times of rapid change, open systems are always more flexible, resilient and propulsive; they offer the chance to feel and respond first to change. So Web People favor more trade expansion, along the lines of the Trans-Pacific Partnership, and more managed immigration that attracts the most energetic and smartest minds, and more vehicles for lifelong learning.

Web People also understand that while we want to prevent another bout of recklessness on Wall Street, we don't want to choke off risk-taking, which is the engine of growth and entrepreneurship.

In the case of Democracy Earth and Santi, blockchain technology is key to the empowerment and propagation of the beliefs held by web people. I asked him to share his future vision for the implementation of decentralised technology (blockchain specifically) and what that might look like. What does he think the future of jurisdiction will look like in that context?

The example of Bitcoin and where it points towards for the future of politics

Let me give you an example that relates to my personal life. Being in Argentina 4-5 years ago, our currency was facing very high inflation, around 30-40% annual inflation rate. We didn't have ability to buy foreign currency of any kind, so you were stuck with monopoly money, and out of the blue

*comes this technology called Bitcoin that suddenly
gets you connected to global commerce. And it
becomes more and more valuable as time goes by
and it's pushed by network effects. I published this
original paper on breaking central authority and
also this piece of technology that is disruptive of
the building blocks of every single element of
modern financial institutions: that is currency.*

*Coming from Argentina it's like a no brainer. I faced
hyperinflation, I faced banks stealing the savings of
citizens. Every single kind of financial crisis you can
imagine, and finally comes this technology that
takes power out of corporate and greedy
institutions.*

*This technology won't stop. The Pandora's Box has
been opened and it will keep on growing and it will
keep on figuring out how to scale and figuring how
to have a larger amount of impact. And it's really a
very empowering tool. I had no option 4-5 years
ago to buy US dollars or to buy anything that made
my money worth something. With technology you
have this permissionless network that's the internet
that doesn't look at who you are when you
implement new stuff, and we have already figured
out a way of doing currency in a borderless,*

trustless way, and it's just a matter of time how we figure out how to do all the other stuff too.

How we do governance, how we do digital institutions, and I think that's one of the most exciting fields in technology right now and also one of the most exciting things in politics. The things about politics is that 100% of the political debate is completely ignorant about this. They are just simply not able to grasp what all of this means. I think that that inevitability of the impact of this technology is really there and I think that a lot of us - here in Silicon Valley, but anywhere in the world really, are contributing to this mission.

Governance and how we organise the planet

This felt like a good time to explore the issue of representatives that we touched on earlier and discussed extensively with Adam and MiVote. I was keen to get Santi's thoughts on how we saw this playing out.

Me

It's interesting that you talk about professional politicians being ignorant of this inevitable transition. I'm wondering what's your view on what

*the future of governance is. You mentioned
governance - this technology bypasses the idea of
representation, so what do you think the future of
governance does look like?*

Santi
*There are many interesting ideas out there and I
think we have to see the implementations and how
they turn out to work. Certainly the way we do
institutions right now resembles how central power
operates - in a way that institutions have a CEO, or
a president; they have a board, or a congress; they
have electoral processes. Those have been the
practices in the modern world for the last 200
years. But the internet have led to a couple
interesting things. It just has broken every single
rule in the book. One is free software or open
source software. The possibility of generating
extremely valuable technology without being
necessarily organised as a corporation or having
funding, or being related to a capitalistic process of
any kind.*

*Free software is really something that broke every
rule in the book on how you create technology. I
think that looking forward, definitely that will also
have an impact on how we create institutions, how*

we wrap the institutions that build these technologies. Institutions relied historically on banks and government, but now the internet offers a new route, and this new route has to do with these technologies that are emerging right now, like they are taking advantage of very recent innovations in cryptography starting from Satoshi Nakamoto onwards - that have to do with the idea of blockchains, the idea of the Bitcoin, the idea of smart contracts, and are also building blocks to new ways of governance that will have to test and iterate in new directions. There is the idea of liquid democracy.

There is also another interesting innovation that turned everything upside down: Wikipedia. The notion that we have about authority right now is completely different from the notion that we had back in the 90's. Wikipedia is like this incredibly democratic experiment.

The interesting thing is that when these things happen throughout history, all the time there was a disruption in information technology. There is the same thing that happened with the printing press 500 years ago. Initially, Gutenberg's bible tried to look as much as possible at the official bibles from the church and eventually that led to folkloric language, that led to new imagined communities, and eventually that led to new kinds of encyclopedias and new notions on what knowledge is valuable to power. Wikipedia changed a lot of our notions of authority. I think that Wikipedia and open source are first steps towards building a planetary commerce with the internet.

The network is our new sovereign

There's a lot of interest certainly on understanding what all of these things mean for democracy, but another way of framing this is through the concept of sovereignty. What it means to be sovereign.

There's a german philosopher from the 30's, probably not ideologically good to quote because he was somewhat related to the Nazi's, but he's called Carl Schmitt. A very good thinker. He has very interesting ideas on political theory. He has a quote that I really like, he says that, "Sovereign is he who decides to be the exception."

That's a sovereign moment - being able to choose to be the exception. Throughout history we've had three kinds of sovereignties. The tribal sovereignty, where you have a tribe and you either belong (or not) to that tribe. We've had the kings, where you are loyal to the king or not. And now we have the corporate state, where you are a member of a nation or not. The network itself is the the new kind of sovereign entity that we are heading towards as we develop these technologies.

It's the case for myself that I told you about with Bitcoin. I was able to leave my country, empty wallet, and arrive to the United States with all my funds because i turned all my cash into Bitcoin and then when I arrived to the US, all my Bitcoin is there waiting for me in America. That kind of possibility has only been possible to extremely powerful people in the past, or extremely powerful organisations. But suddenly an individual being able to do that... I recently talked with a Venezuelan activist and he told me that (which is a bad side effect of all of this) most people who were selling Bitcoin in Venezuela left the country.

That new sovereign entity at the individual, personal level... it's very, very interesting and as we find ways to do more sustainable energy, and as the cost of solar keeps going down, as technology keeps democratizing... at the end, the bottom line of it is really about the machine to machine economy and I think that we can really start empowering people in completely new ways.

Democracy Earth

Me

Tell me a little bit more about Democracy Earth and the different products and experimentations that you're going through at the moment to make this world you describe become reality.

Santi

With Democracy Earth, what we're doing right now is looking at two key things. One is liquid democracy - we have been conducting research for over a year now in different locations around the world, we have a very good partner for that, but unfortunately I cannot disclose that! But we have been testing with different communities in different contexts, prototypes that specifically look at the right kind of user experience to do delegation of trust online.

At the same time, we have been working with researchers at the University of Berkeley to understand how the leadership that happens offline is properly marked on the online tool or vice versa. There are many issues about liquid democracy - delegation of power is not something that a lot of people like to do sometimes... depends on the topic. We're doing a lot of research in that field.

Blockchain democratising the auditing of votes

On the other hand, is figuring out from the back-end perspective, how we can use blockchain-based technology to store this information and to make this information accountable and transparent. One of the most interesting elements of working with blockchain specifically for democracy, is that it really democratises the one element that is not possible to democratise, and that's the auditing of the votes. Being able to to get everyone to count the votes without requiring any kind of 'special access' to our servers or to our infrastructure, or to the headquarters of the government.

By storing information directly on a blockchain, every voter gets the right to see the vote of every other voter. There are other concerns as well, regarding secrecy of the vote and other challenges, from the cryptographic perspective there are really a lot of considerations to be made, because these kinds of systems do get attacked and the right cryptography has to be put in place. But the implications of a decent try at democracy are incredible, and the best thing is that once you have the technology, that technology can be implemented anywhere, at any scale. Small organisations, large organisations, entire nations, the whole world or just your home town. In that sense it can be a very subversive piece of technology.

So there are two ways of subverting a democracy - gossip and identity. Blockchains store the facts directly. There was a Venezuelan activist working in Caracas, a very well known activist, 300,000 followers on Twitter (his platform to do activism is Twitter), a working class guy, and he asked me, "Santiago, what is politics to you?" *and I remember I answered with a cliche,* "the art of the impossible" *or some kind of crap like that and he said,* "no, no, no, politics is one thing and one thing only: What you say at a given point in time. That's politics." *A blockchain, ultimately, is a tool for recording what has been said at a given point in time, without relying on central authority. It's automates that. Historically we needed notaries, we needed*

lawyers, accountants, politicians, to certify and
verify information. All of those actors being human,
they had an incentive, sometimes, to deceive the
system and to lie about it. By automating the
storing of facts on a decentralised ledger, then it
really can...

We've spoken a lot about decentralisation, and in my
offline conversations about this, the one thing that comes
up time and time again is safety and subversion. I think
that many people have a naive perspective that the
current electoral system can't be subverted because
paper is traceable. Of course this is untrue. You just know
if it's been subverted or not. So I wanted to touch a little
more on this with Santi who said the following:

The main problem with democracy is... there are
two ways you can subvert a democracy. One is if
you are able to control the identities that get the
right to vote. That's what's known in cryptographic
literature as a 'sybil attack'. A sybil attack is faking
or forging an identity or a network or any context
that is used for the accountability of the process.
Most of the hacks on democracies are usually
hacks on the identities that get the right to vote. A
typical attack, "let's put the dead people on the
registry to vote and have someone to vote on their

behalf." *That actually happens a lot - faking
identities and the sybil attack is the main way to
subvert it. Another way you can subvert a
democracy is with gossip - with false information.
By inflicting gossip in a context you can really run
the show in any way you want to. Lies really get
very far.*

As we just discussed and as we will touch upon in the e-
Estonian example, the blockchain largely cuts this
problem out because it can be the ledger for digital
identities. So identity theft is far less feasible in this
structure. But Santi's next point is far more chilling:

> *I think that the main thing that needs to be battled
> in a democracy, is gossip running the show. When
> you look at political rhetoric, anywhere in world , it's
> really about... everything politicians do is to
> discredit, systematically, discredit the other side, all
> the time. That's all that politicians do. They
> discredit the other side all the time, in order to
> pursue their own personal interests. And that's
> what leads to lies running the whole show, and lies
> are the first steps to corruption. Blockchains really
> put a much higher hurdle for that kind of
> manipulation to happen. I think that in that respect,
> there's a lot of beauty to be explored in*

*decentralised ways of governance. But there are
also new ways that these systems can be gamed
and we need to research, to look into them and see
how it is.*

Gossip and stories are the most prevalent forms of
gaming that we see in politics historically speaking but I
believe that a combination of the points we've discussed
make this extremely difficult in the future. The blockchain
is one thing, but there are others. The nuanced voting
from pol.is makes it very difficult for one particular
ideology to rule. The destinational frames and direct
policy voting with MiVote, also make this very hard. The
thing is with digital direct and distributed democracy, the
conversation shifts entirely from the personalities to the
policies, and whilst I'm sure in the future, politicians or
other parties with interest will find ways of gaming the
system, it will be tougher if the conversation isn't about
them.

Finally, I wanted to know how Santi sees the future of
governance and as the pragmatic philosopher he seems
to be, this was his answer:

Planetary Governance

I'm all in for the idea of turning the internet into a planetary jurisdiction that can operate anywhere in the world and really address the challenges of the 21st century. With the fall of the Berlin Wall in 1989, it really didn't end it there, that was just the first step in a greater political trend and has to do with the decline of nation states and fictional borders and or dividing us. I think that the fall of the Berlin Wall was very symbolic, but it was just the beginning. Maybe Brexit is another chapter in that greater arc of fragmentation that leads towards greater decentralisation but ultimately, towards ending nation states entirely.

As we are being more connected as a digital society anywhere in the world, that becomes each day, much more a certain possibility. The importance of Bitcoin, the importance of much of this technology, the importance of the internet won't stop at the cultural level. Every single information technology in the past, ultimately will change the core dynamics of institutions. Just like the printing press brought the modern republic. That's what I'm in for. Figuring out how we can think planetary governance with the internet and blockchains in the 21st century.

'planetary governance with the internet and blockchains in the 21st century', 'ending nation states entirely', 'digital society', 'planetary jurisdiction'... These are the kinds of visionary ideas that the revolutionary people I've spoken are contemplating and prototyping solutions for, yet they are absent in the mainstream political discourse and largely absent in the media. This disparity between the visions of what I believe to be incredibly smart, pragmatic and active people vs the majority of the political elite, is why the cover of this book is red. Because the old and the new are on very different pages and historically when that gap gets too big, we end up with placards and anthems. This is why I think this is a revolution:

So, in summary, here is what I think are the main takeaways from our internet philosopher, Santiago Siri, and planetary revolution that starts with Democracy Earth:

Digital direct democracy: we've discussed how technology makes the notion of true direct democracy possible and Democracy Earth makes this idea super tangible. Voting directly on policy is possible through a simple voting mechanism. Is there any need for politicians anymore?!

Change from inside the system: Unfortunately, the current system isn't ready for this, so the only way to make the people's decisions count for something was to create a dummy party inside the parliament that could follow the request of citizens. An interesting and innovative way to work within the constraints of an existing system.

Informal governmental accountability: If changing the system from the inside still doesn't get big enough results, putting politicians under pressure is made possible by making the electorates expressed needs visible publicly. This mean any subsequent discord between what people want and what politicians do is also visible.

And so as Santi has brought up these ideas of nation states ending and planetary governance, it felt right to follow his thinking on with a very tangible story. e-Estonia is a project which has challenged my perspective on what a country is and what that could mean for governance, geography and society at large. Here we go...

Estonian e-Residency

Key principles

Citizen centricity and government as a company

Feedback over voting to change legislation

Borderless & competing nations

It's not where you were born and what race you are, but what are your values and where do you want to belong, and choosing your kind of nation according to your values, not place of birth.

- Kaspar Korjus

Estonia e-Residency in a nutshell

This, and the example of the UK's Government Digital Service are the only initiatives in the book that emerge out of official governments. Estonia have been the nippy speedboat in this sea of sluggish oil tankers, taking their existing digital infrastructures and making them available to the whole world.

The result of this is the Estonian e-Residency platform. A system by which foreigners can be Estonian e-Residents, benefiting from great digital public services, from digital identification, the ability to setup up location-independent businesses easily, and crucial banking and taxation services.

There are, at the time of writing (November 2016, but head to their 'dashboard' to see live stats) 13,500 e-residents of Estonia. They've achieved this growth rapidly and effectively by thinking like a startup. Estonian e-Residency is a startup of 7 people punching way above their weight on a global scale by building their services according to the same mindsets and attitudes that the world's most innovative startups have. They constantly ask for user feedback, they ship quickly and iterate.

Why is this interesting?

Citizen centricity and Nation State as a Service

The Estonian e-Residency project doesn't operate from old mental models which see a clear divide between companies and government. To them a user is a user, a citizen is a customer, and the only way is to serve them.

Feedback over voting to change legislation

This citizen-centric approach is seen very clearly in just how much they ask for feedback. To the extent that it wasn't even clear what the platform would be until they asked people to sign up and tell them what they needed. This constant feedback loop has resulted in the creation or amendment of 5 different pieces of Estonian legislation in just one year. Here, feedback is a way faster and more powerful tool for citizen participation than voting itself.

Borderless & competing nations

This is evident in the way they describe their business model. Their shareholders are the taxpayers, therefore they need to help their taxpayers earn good money so that in turn they can have benefit from the taxes necessary to keep doing good work. In their view, if you don't provide the best experience for your citizens they will leave and join other countries becoming e-residents there instead.

Before hearing from the Estonian e-Residency project, here is some context for this interview by evolutionary historian and author of *'Sapiens'*, Yuval Harari:

> *As the twenty-first century unfolds, nationalism is fast losing ground. More and more people believe that all of humankind is the legitimate source of political authority, rather than the members of a particular nationality, and that safeguarding human rights and protecting the interests of the entire human species should be the guiding light of politics. If so, having close to 200 independent states is a hinderance rather than a help. Since Swedes, Indonesians and Nigerians deserve the same human rights, wouldn't it be simpler for a single global government to safeguard them?*

> *Immensely powerful currents of capital, labour and information turn and shape the world, with a growing disregard for the borders and opinions of states.*

> *The global empire being forged before our eyes is not governed by any particular state or ethnic group. It is ruled by a multi-ethnic elite, and is held together by a common culture and common interests. Throughout the world, more and more*

entrepreneurs, engineers, experts, scholars, lawyers and managers are called to join the empire. They must ponder whether to answer the imperial call or to remain loyal to their state and their people. More and more choose the empire.
- *'Sapiens: A Brief History of Humankind'* by Yuval Harari

Estonia e-Residency in their own words

I spoke to the Managing Director of Estonia's e-Residency project Kaspar Korjus, and asked him how he got involved:

I'm managing director of e-Residency at the moment. I started being involved with e-Estonia things five years ago. I was studying abroad in Lancaster in the UK, and for 4 years I was there and then there was the residency programme and they were kind enough to invite me back to Estonia, and then two years ago, I got an offer from the CIO of Estonia, Taavi Kotka, to try out one scholarship about e-Residency.

It's early to stop on this, but following on from Santi's comments about a new generation of millennials changing democracy, it's worth noting that Kaspar became Managing Director following a scholarship. In other words, the person that the government of Estonia has chosen to lead this revolutionary project isn't a politician or somebody with a long CV, because he simply doesn't have that many years behind him. He's a young guy with knowledge and experience in the world that we live in, who is shaping the world of tomorrow. This sets the scene for the kind of approach that Estonia have to building a culture of political innovation. Back to Kaspar:

At that point in time I still had my last job, but the very first day when I started to run this e-Residency, we managed to get huge attraction to our landing page, and we got 4,000 subscribers internationally who wanted to become e-Residents of Estonia within a day. So suddenly I realised that this is a much bigger and much more promising topic than we first thought. They initially only considered e-Residency as a column for startups because they knew there is some business behind that. But they didn't really know exactly who the customer was, what the value is in that for them, and why Estonia should do it in the first place.

This approach of launching a product or service before it even really exists is quite common amongst fast moving startups. Apparently when Steve Jobs set up NeXT he went as far as unveiling their beautiful black cube without it even having a functioning operating system. The most famous and illustrative example of this however is Dropbox. Their CEO and founder Drew Houston wanted to check if the world was interested in the product before making it. So instead of investing hundreds of hours in designing and coding the product, then waiting on tenterhooks to see if anyone bought it, he made a 3-minute video demonstration of how it would work and put it online. According to Houston it drove hundreds of thousands of people to the website, and the beta waiting list skyrocketed to 75,000 people. In 2014, Dropbox was valued at $10 billion, a living testament to the lean startup approach. An approach which e-Estonia adopts, like most good startups, the difference here being that they are a startup inside a government, and that is the innovation here. Kaspar continues the story:

> *Throughout that last two years, we have e-residents internationally telling us what they want, how they want us to support them, and we have changed the laws accordingly, we have developed new services and changed the processes. So now, if people want to become e-residents, they used to have to grab a flight to Estonia, now they can apply online and have a face-to-face meeting and give their fingerprints in any Estonian foreign embassy. Then they receive the identify card. We changed many laws...*

What I'd like to pull out here, is again this notion of citizen centricity. The Estonian project really deeply 'involves' its citizens in its process. The services were created and built as a response to listening to the real expressed needs of their users (internally, they use the same language as any startup, 'users', rather than citizens). They then iterate not only the services as quickly as possible, but also the country's legislation to accommodate for the best user experience possible. Groundbreaking work from what is essentially a public institution.

We'll come back to the legal aspects of this in a bit, but first, a little more about what Estonian e-Residency is, how it works and why it's interesting for e-residents. Here are the principles benefits of Estonian e-Residency which Kaspar outlined.

Location independent business environment & banking

So the main thing, why people become e-residents today is for business reasons, and the main value for them is the location independent business environment, the EU business environment, which you can establish within a day. You establish bank accounting in a day, get access to payment providers like Paypal, set up the whole package which helps you to be this digital nomad, to work anywhere in the world while at the same time having access to all the digital services and at the same time, being able to digitally sign contracts and everything else.

We are now getting ready to open bank accounts online for e-residents. It's taken a while because the longest law that we changed was the banking law. This took exactly two years, and by July we changed the law and in the coming weeks the first banks are enabling onboarding, and that was the last milestone. E-residents used to actually have to visit the EU and now they don't have to, yet they have the advantages of EU business around them.

It's especially attractive to the UK at the moment, because of Brexit. Lots of questions regarding, "does it solve the issue if you came in not part of the EU" and then because of lots of enquiries we even built a separate planning page for Brexit people: "How to stay in the EU" etc... and there, basically, you have all the information - how you can establish EU co-operation whilst still living in the UK and having access to all the EU business environments, including banking giros, fintech passporting services and everything else, and it's very cost effective. So this really made sense and then just last week 'The Guardian' wrote an article about that and we got 600 extra applications from the UK interested about that. So technically we can see one value that being part of the EU gives us, in the business market, technical data and not only the UK, but for Estonian emerging markets also.

The second value proposition for e-residence is access to financial services. For Brexit people, of course, they already have it, but most of the people internationally don't have it. They can't sell services on the internet because they can't accept foreign currencies. They can't build up websites where people can pay by credit cards. So with e-Residency - we verify who you are on the internet and that's why you can now have access to those financial services even if your residency comes from a market which is not recognised in financial markets internationally.

The third valuable proposition is that it has environmental and location independence - you don't need to be connected to one country anymore to run your business. You can work one month in Malaysia, another in Silicon Valley and another in Europe and still run everything from cloud, so that you don't need to hire any local *managers or directors or give power of attorney to anyone because you yourself can be the owner of the company and just digitally sign everything.*

This starts to touch upon the notions of geography that Santi started addressing when he spoke of planetary jurisdiction and governance. This is the 'web utopia' that many digital fanatics believe in, at least philosophically or spiritually. It questions the notion of a nation, the idea of which countries we belong to, of nationality, of every assumption we have attached to ownership and borders. This is the 'Webs vs Walls' that Thomas Friedman spoke of, in practice. Kaspar puts it like this:

In the future, the big picture is that we are building towards a new nation state which is fully digital, fully transparent, fully legitimate, which empowers its citizens and gives access to all the services like nations states do, but to everybody... including education, healthcare, business environments and everything else. But today because our team is just 7 people, we are concentrating only on the business environment and offering value there.

That's right. Only 7 people did all this.

This question of a new type of nation state is something I had thought of in an abstract way and termed '#hashtags vs hierarchies' but speaking to Kaspar was the first time this really made sense to me in practice, concretely. I asked him to flesh this out. What might the country of the future look like? How do countries interact with one another? How do they interact with other types of organisations like companies?

> *The fully digital, fully transparent, fully inclusive nation state which would invite every person, every member to be part of this... fully legitimate which means that there are those digital nation states - I don't want to name them - which are on islands or are on cloud, but don't have the jurisdiction, they don't have legislation behind that, and that's why everything we do... you are part of anti-money laundering), you're part of the banking laws, you're part of the digital single market, e-digital signature, etc... So everything is part of this new nation, as you join that.*

> *It's empowering because most people, even if you have internal taxes, this is not enough... if you're on the internet, you're still a no-one, still no-one can recognise you. So that's why we say that e-residents are empowered through digital identities.*

And the fully digital in that sense means that it gives location independence.

The broader picture is that as a government, e-Residency is not a new initiative in that sense, it's still on the infrastructure that Estonia has been functioning with already for 15/17 years - it's the nation state that manages to exchange data between parties, and the private and public sector in a private and a secure way, so that most of the transactions are done behind the scenes. For example if e-residents want to clear taxes then automatically, e-residents can give access to their income, to their property, to their children and everything else and the tax office calculates everything for them, they just need to digitally sign and accept the declaration. Because the digital communication works here.

That's why Estonia is able to scale those services to foreigners and and offer it everybody and open it up, and that's why for Estonia, the big picture is that although in the physical life we do need borders, because we're part of the EU world, in the digital life, we don't need borders. We can offer all of our services to everybody and doesn't even add too much extra cost because we need to develop those services anyway, we need a business environment, we need banking laws, we need the services anyway, and just now, we want to enable everybody to be part of that.

This strategy is underpinned by internet logic. As John Buck put it, *"there is no geography on the internet"* and this is clear here, as Estonia, a small country of only 1 million people, is able to open up its services to the whole world. 'Software as a Service' (SaaS) is a commonly used term for this business model, and again, the innovation here is that it is applied to a country. What Kaspar aptly calls Nation State as a Service (NSaaS). This is super interesting because it means that in this particular case, Estonia e-Residency is a competitor to Stripe Atlas, a US tech company which allows people to setup a business in the US. Countries and competition competing with one another.

Nation State as a Service (NSaaS)

The definition of 'country' changes. Usually 'country' means that you have some residents and citizens there, but for us, everybody can be part of the country and we can see there's no other way in the future, because the next country... if they are not going to offer their services to everybody then they will lose this game.

Because the product development is the same - as in a startup. Imagine two people making the same product, but one is just targeting to 1 million people, and the other is targeting to 1 billion people. The first one just eventually can't win because their product development costs the same for 1 million people. Other nations are going to follow and to offer their services to everybody and then we can see the different nation states are going to compete or collaborate together to offer the best 'digital nation states as a service to citizens' and everybody can opt in or opt out of different governments who offer their services.

And just today basically, the market is so free that as a nation state we can offer everything because no one is offering it. In 10 years time definitely, there are 10 different e-Residencies and you can choose: "perhaps I do business in this environment in Asia, business in that e-Residency in Europe, or health care in that e-Residency scheme in Cuba, or whatever." *Then you have different kinds of services from different governments offered to you.*

But the foundation of all of this is two main things -

*the nation state has to be able to recognise 'who
we are' to offer those services - that can be done
only if we have strong digital identities. The second
thing is that they need to be able to offer you
services so that data can be exchanged between
each other and between governments. That means
an infrastructure layer of data exchange which in
Estonia is called 'X-Road'.*

Estonia is pioneering in its use of digital identities, and
this is also something that Santi touched upon earlier.
Again, the Blockchain is one of the technologies that
could make this truly possible whilst avoiding corruption
or identity theft.

*Eventually we will have a world where nation states
are not monopolistic anymore, competition is there
and if you don't offer the best user experience to
your citizens, residents and e-residents, but your
neighbouring country does, then you will lose your
market inside your country. That's pretty amazing
because everybody is eventually fed up of bad
government service and perhaps that can change.*

We've touched on the startup mentality that Kaspar and
his team have but this last point reframed something for
me. He sees countries just as most people see

companies. They exist to provide great service. If they don't do that, their customers will leave. This has been possible only by emigrating in the past but in the future we may start seeing forms of 'digital emigration'. In the same way that the rich put their money in remote tax havens, this could be the case for almost anything that we traditionally depend on our countries for.

For instance, if we think of how quickly 'healthtech' and 'edtech' are progressing, we could consider a future where our country's national physical health system has to compete with healthtech companies or even with other digital nations. Countries and companies compete or collaborate alike online, which is why building a digital nation as a platform makes so much sense. The digital nation becomes a platform for apps to plug into, for startups to add services to...etc.

> *We don't call people 'citizens' anymore. For us they are all customers. We want to attract customers. To attract more customers we need to have good legislation, user friendly services, we need to treat them well - like any startup. As a government, we can't see that differently to the private sector, like a government normally would. But whatever it does, it needs to offer a good service and our goal is 10 million e-residents by 2025, and that is exactly what*

we see as a customer base and we work every day to attract more customers.

I think there will be some clear aspects of what the nation state provides to you, like identity, like some basic things, but I think most of the things, as nation states are opening their services to everybody - nation states will be seen as quite similar to private sector companies. If one service provider who offers one kind of service to me as a person, the service can be a citizenship service, the service can be an identity service and I can choose that if I want to, and there are ways to get that if I want to, but it is just another service provider.

With this in mind, I wanted to know more about how Kaspar sees the similarities and differences between countries and companies, particularly when it comes to money and business models:

There are two aims I would say. One thing to consider is that my salary comes from the public sector which means that my shareholder is the Estonian tax payer, which means that I need to please the Estonian tax payer, which means that they need to earn some money.

So there needs to be this business model in place so that our shareholder will continue funding us. The business model is that the Estonian private sector offer services to e-residents - banking services, physical addresses for a company, banking advice, legal advice etc. So there is a new ecosystem of services that we can offer to e-residents... it can be healthcare and all other services. And then, this brings in new money to the country, and this means that the Estonian private sector will pay more taxes because they get more money, then eventually, we as a government will get more money because the Estonian private sector is better off. There is also 10% of e-residents who sometimes pay taxes directly to Estonia but that is not the business model and that means that we don't take tax revenues if these people don't live at all in Estonia, and their jurisdiction says "you should pay in your own country."

This virtuous circle business model is something that is also concurrent with modern business logic. It creates what is sometimes referred to as a 'lock-on' where the service is so good that customers are incentivised to stay in the system and the revenue per customer increases. The most famous example of this is probably Apple, whose closed ecosystem thrives from each new product adding value to the existing ones. Financially, the business model here makes common sense, but applied to a government this feels very progressive to me. They understand that if their services aren't good, people will leave. We already see a lot of this in Europe where there is an increasing trend of creatives leaving big established financial and business-focused cities like London, for cheaper, more innovative cities like Budapest, Chiang Mai, Prague, Bangkok, Taipei, Ubud, Porto, Berlin, etc (see nomadlist.com) where they can get the same or better services at a cheaper price.

I wanted to know more about Kaspar's view on the changing and developing relationships between countries. I was also curious to learn more about how he saw the evolution of nations specialising in certain areas (e.g. Silicon Valley to raise money, Cayman Islands to hide money, Singapore to protect IP, Switzerland to protect money).

> *There is a book on my reading list, it has this story that the borders today won't have such importance in the future, but instead of borders there will be direct links, and direct links are in between major cities, and cities will have dominance, and cities have been the dominant nodes in the global*

network for a long time. Countries come and go but cities remain and the collaboration between cities will have higher impact. Let's say Singapore, Silicon Valley, Tallinn, for example, they each can give something to this network, and the way these systems are interoperable, and how users can choose and be part of those three 'halves; and how they can work together... I think this is very important and very useful. Then it's less about borders and more about linkages.

Each country needs to find the thing which they're they best at. You can't be best at everything, like today. You can't be the best at IP protection and have best business environment etc... you go have your holidays in Brazil and you keep your IP in Singapore, you do your business to Estonia and you get fundraising in Silicon Valley. Each city or country needs to find what it's the best at and then scale it to international level. Like you do with startups. You find which problem you can't solve today and then solve it and offer the solution to everybody. In the same way that, today, inside one country it makes sense.

We have things like: "this cluster is the best in industry, in Denver, in the US, let's say, it's best for incorporation." *There are different parts inside the country, but so far globalisation hasn't taken that effect that the country becomes the best at something then offers it to everybody else outside the country, as we have seen in the rare cases of our e-residency or Singapore. I think the importance for governments is to recognise this but not to copy others. What can they be the best at? What can they offer to the global ecosystem, so that they can outsource everything else, and just concentrate on the things they are the best at and scale that thing and become much wealthier, rather than trying to solve all of the problems for citizens themselves.*

As the conversation developed, we discussed the motivations behind these kinds of models. Namely, that most businesses exist solely to make money, so what about countries who traditionally, are there to serve the people of their country?

The other reason and motivation behind this is doing 'good' in that sense. We have a platform that enables us to speak with people every day and understand how much they are struggling in the business world. And for us if it doesn't cost anything, it feels like more of an obligation to open these kind of things for foreigners, also for other people in emerging markets especially. You help them, especially if it also makes Estonia richer, then there are no conflicts and we can just be there and help each other.

More importantly, it's not where you were born and what race you are, but what are your values and where do you want to belong, and choosing your kind of nation according to your values, not place of birth.

I think this will leave the possibility that we don't all need to be the same and we don't all need to accept each other if we don't want to. But at least we can be part of those communities both physically and digitally, where we want to belong and where we feel better and where we feel one of them.

It's great to see Estonia as a tangible example of how equality and the internet's role in improving this is possible. Location-independent business doesn't only mean that 'digital nomads' can work from beaches in Bali. It also means that people in emerging markets have access to great online services and can have a digital identity and therefore a digital legitimacy. They can run their business so long as they have an internet connection.

Estonia has tried to find it's own 'Nokia', because Finland had Nokia for 20 years. How can we be useful for the ecosystem, and now through these last years, Estonia's found a 'Nokia' in e-Residency. Some countries offer 'trying to do world peace' internationally, and we are trying to empower citizens internationally through technology, which we have. We have that capability and we can do that so that's how we can see that. Although perhaps we're a bit naive, we think we can actually be helpful in the global ecosystem.

Estonia seem to have found their specialism and niche, and are pioneers who are 'first to market' when it comes to being a digital nation state. So finally, I asked Kaspar what he thought the future of democracy looked like, and particularly what he thought of representation and voting as a democratic system. In his answer he talks about user feedback as an equal if not higher impact form of involvement than the traditional vote, and how this has led them to change several laws in just a few months:

Sometimes e-residents ask if they can vote for laws in Estonia, or people ask "when can the e-residents

start voting? when do they have rights to vote?"
*because today they don't have. And my usual
answer is that I feel today that e-residents are more
part of our society than residents and citizens
today, because the residents and citizens can vote
once every four years in some elections.*

*From e-residents, we ask for different feedback
every day. We give them priorities with what we are
doing - we are offering to rank them, we are making
computations and according to those, already we
have changed five or six laws in one year. We have
changed the process of how they get what they
want, we have developed new services for what
they want so this is taking feedback from e-
residents and they're telling us what laws we
should change, and we change them.*

*And those guys who change the laws, those
politicians, or whatever we call them today, they are
employees or administrators who make them
happen. Today different ministries are working with
you, but they still don't consider you as one user,
because as a user you may want your health care,
and you want to use perhaps the business
environment or some other product, but there are
two different persons with whom you need to*

speak.

As e-residents, if we take user perspective, then you have one contact person. Then you have direct access to give us feedback about our relations and everything we need to change. So this is the first point to take - voting itself seems like such an old school way of how you can be part of democracy because financially it doesn't matter anyway, who is in charge of something. What matters is the vision and the digital country that you are building can be built together with users and with direct feedback.

The second half of the answer is how the system can be different in the future... Definitely there will be some conflicts because if there are 10 million e-residents and 1 million residents in Estonia, then the question comes, "why can't they officially vote in our elections if they contribute more to our economy than residents? And why, who and which residents have that privilege to take that money that e-residents bring in?" *I think there definitely will be that kind of context there, in their future, but I'm not a kind of 'new world global citizen' who believes that in the next 20-40 years the country itself will change so dramatically that the political systems will change, or the voting systems, or the way politicians are represented. I think this will remain, and residents and citizens will all have more rights to become actively engaged in the decision making process.*

Governments are getting better at serving their residents and e-residents internationally, and the people will become more involved in policy-making processes and more part of this, so that you don't feel that there are some 'guys' who make decisions for you but through technology, people feel that they can actually actively and directly contribute to all the services and policy making processes.

This point to me totally encapsulates what it means and could mean to really seriously adopt some of the organisational principles we discussed in Part 2, to a government. Feedback as a vote is the simplest yet one of the most innovative things I've heard so far and with several laws changing due to that feedback, it can be extremely impactful.

The notion of a nation could be about to change.

So, in summary, here are the big points I took out of my conversation with Kaspar and the Estonian E-residency platform:

Citizen centricity and Nation State as a Service
The digital nation state lives and dies by the service
it gives to its users.

Feedback over voting to change legislation
How a digital nation state incorporates feedback,
all the way to changing legislation is a fast and
effective way of creating customer centric change.

Borderless & competing nations
The concept of what a country is and the
relationship between it and other organisations,
including other countries, could be about to
become a lot more dynamic.

insights
& takeaways

You will have formed your own insights, inspiration and objections to these stories and to different parts of this book. My perspective is by now pretty clear, but I'd like to conclude these stories with my takeaways and thoughts.

To me, the stories of these exponential thinkers are a form of hope in the potential for genuine reform at a deeper and more fundamental level than childish political heckling. To me, these stories offer an image of what the future could look like and although, like any system, it will still have many flaws, I believe this will be a better future.

Putting these different pieces of puzzle together, shows us a lot of overlap which we covered theoretically in Parts 1 and 2, as well as some complimentary distinctions between the different approaches currently being taken. Let's take a little look at this.

What do they all have in common?

None of them are professional politicians. They are all

291

techies and/or entrepreneurs to some degree. Considering Kaspar's comment that *"nation states will be seen as quite similar to private sector companies"*, this isn't surprising. To me this is less about the formal organisational structures they're a part of, and more about their attitudes and beliefs. As discussed in the setup, they all display a different approach to the traditional industrial government or organisational models when it comes to:

- **failure:** all adopted lean and agile processes and saw failure as the premise for improvement

- **distribution of power:** all involved many people in their process and rather than focus on powerful people, they created powerful processes

- **openness with information:** all totally opened up their process or platform (in some cases even the financial details)

- **listening to people:** all built their platforms with the people for which the platform is intended

- **radical reform:** all have created systems which are radically different on a systemic level, these aren't iterative improvements on the existing system but rather totally new models for governance

- no border mentality / non dualistic: all of them believe in cross-border collaboration to the point where they don't necessarily believe in borders themselves, there is no nationalism or divisive rhetoric to be seen in their stories, they see one humanity

- technology as a philosophy: all of them understand the philosophies which underpin internet logic and decentralised governance based on principles such as open source, distributed authority, web thinking, and failure as a learning opportunity

- values driven: all of them talk about the higher human needs they are looking to fulfil, the fundamental human values they are driven by, and not their own success

- tech adopters: of course they were all picked because of this, it is the premise of the book, but it's worth noting that blockchain and machine learning feature heavily. Two reasonably new technologies (in their evolved forms at least) applied to a sector which tends to evolve at a dead snail's pace.

What is complimentary about these different perspectives?

As I spoke to each of them, I started seeing connections between different stories and thought *"oh that would go well with that thing that that other project is doing"*. If ever a country were to wholesale adopt these disruptive forms of democracy, I can see how different elements from these projects could easily complement one another.

For instance: it isn't inconceivable that a nation could crowdsource a constitution (like Iceland), and involve its e-residents (like Estonia) in that process to foster collaboration from across the world (using pol.is to power those conversations). Once that constitution is implemented, more specific decisions could be made by adopting a destinational approach (like MiVote) where citizens could deliberate before making their decisions or even propose new approaches (like DemocracyOS).

In fact, I don't actually see much contradiction between these different approaches. I find this incredibly energising to think that all of these different approaches could support each other to create the deepest form of democracy.

So what is the role of representatives in this future world?

Well, I'm still not quite sure. I see little need for ultimate leadership from something like a Prime Minister, but I do see a huge huge role for deliberation and implementation. The role shifts from decision makers, to facilitators of the decision making process. Good facilitation by trained facilitators and through machine learning will be essential to support large groups of citizens to move forward. To avoid any sort of corruption, those will most likely have to be rolling positions like jury service is today. Nobody can be a professional, it is all our responsibility to move our society forward. As for implementation, it could still be that we have civil servants implementing the will of the people, but I think this could become the role of organisations. We gave the example of Citymapper earlier, a company which is essentially doing the job of local governments. This could be something we see more and more in the future.

Education Squared

All of this radical change hinges on one huge problem that is, I believe, the root cause of most of the failures of the current democratic system: education. So long as this industrial system continues to impose 'truth' and 'knowledge' on people, limit creativity, tacitly train and promote hierarchy, close our minds and ignore the basic human wisdom that is required to learn to live, I fear we won't see big enough shifts in the behaviour of the adults we become. Navigating an exponentially changing world can't be done in theory, we will learn from feeling the winds of change and building our way into the future. A one size fits all theoretical education system which rewards academia over real world application will hinder, not help us to find the solutions to humanity's biggest challenges.

For this reason, next year, we will be releasing the next book in the 'Squared' series: Education2. An exploration of the most inspiring and progressive forms of education in the world, that we can enhance and scale in the future to liberate people and help our humanity thrive. There is so much amazing stuff happening in that space and we can't wait to get stuck in.

The fractal perspective, once again, offers us a lens through which to see this problem. Schools have teachers, classrooms, subjects, didactic pedagogic methods, set curriculums, and theoretical concepts. Their graduates move to grown-up businesses which have managers, offices, departments, imposed protocols, 5-year plans, and strategic decks. These organisations are governed by governments which have party leaders, divisively designed houses of parliament (the House of Commons in the UK is literally shaped with 'opposition benches'), ministries, party manifestos and empty promises.

Schools	Orgs	Govt
Teachers	Managers	Party leaders
Classrooms	Offices	Houses of parliament
Subjects	Departments	Ministries
Didactic Pedagogy	Protocols	Wedded to ideologies
Set curriculum	5 year plans	Manifestos

The Internet's role and health

It is clear that these systems are operating on belief systems which don't belong to the protagonists of this book. They all have fundamentally different perspectives to this old system. As Santi said earlier: *"the one thing we have that is totally different from previous generations is definitely the internet. We're called millennials, but in our adolescence, it's really the internet that shaped our minds, rather than the year 2000."*

This attitude shift is what allowed these different revolutionaries to do amazing things I have learned so much from. But this thing that shaped our minds, the internet, is the prerequisite for this to continue, and some experts argue it is in danger...

"To those in power, equality feels like oppression"

Somebody smart and anonymous on the internet

saving the internet

My feelings

All of this depends on keeping our internet safe and I think there's an equal amount to be excited and worried about. Before we hear from the best placed person on the planet on this topic, here is my list:

What scares me:
- AI
- Tor
- Massive server farms
- Mass spying
- Censorship
- Monopolies

- Politicians
- Filter bubbles
- Twitter disappearing

What gives me hope:
- AI
- Tor
- Local wireless energy
- Encryption
- 100% internet access
- Startups
- Blockchain
- Millennials
- Mesh networking
- Driverless cars

Words of wisdom from the inventor of the World Wide Web, Sir Tim Berners-Lee

Some us initially had big hopes that the Internet is going to lead to a society in which inequality fades away because everybody has got the same possibilities, everybody has got the same advantages, just starting off connecting themselves to the net.

Guess what? That hasn't happened. In fact, here we are 25 years after the first webpage and a lot of non profits, a lot of governments, are realising that we have a crisis of inequality. So every time people put more powerful things on the web, we actually increase the gap between the haves and the have nots.

Things need to be said explicitly for the internet because the internet gives you a certain power that you wouldn't have had before. As people have started to think about access to the internet more as a right, then that begs the question: Ok, should we have a bill of rights for the internet?

Snowden changed that dramatically by putting those revelations onto the table that has really started the conversation and I think we are indebted to Edward Snowden for actually introducing that material in a way that I think nothing else could have done that.

There have always been forces to try to control the internet. When you're a government of a country it's very tempting to want to govern the internet within your country. Trouble is, it doesn't work, because the internet is not a thing of countries. You could certainly, you could put in barrier. You could put in firewalls but as you do that suddenly, your country, your people, your entrepreneurs, your teachers, have all lost their voice.

We have to be reactive when we realise, 'woah! actually this country, or this company has stepped over the mark, we have to immediately take to the streets with placards and shouting.'

So in 10 years time we'll see certain natural progressions, we'll see the internet speeds will be very high so it gets to the point where the internet will be able to carry everything that your eyes can perceive, just as when you listen stereo, the internet can feed you anything your ears can hear, it gets enough fidelity.

Whether the internet is an open space or a closed space, I am not going to predict. It is up to us. It all depends on what we do now. All the decisions we make now.

Sir Tim Berners-Lee, inventor of the World Wide Web
at the World Economic Forum

last words

This book has more long quotes in it that any book you've ever read. The reasons are simple. First of all, stories told by the people involved are more interesting than abstract summaries. Secondly, I am not making anything up, I am citing real people doing real things. I initially tried paraphrasing and summarising the work of others when relevant but to do so felt like bastardising the work of so many amazing people. More importantly though, we now have the internet. All the world's knowledge available for us to curate in our own way, and to form our own thoughts and conclusions.

This is what I have done. Using knowledge and frames I've gathered along my life and referring to the amazing projects and research of some great people, I have put together something that I hope stimulates many of us to action. To take away mental barriers we may have preventing us from creating meaningful change in the world and to stand confidently in a belief that we can each and every one of us contribute to rewiring the world we live in to leave it better than ever.

I started thinking about digital democracy almost 10 years ago, but in the process of writing this book and being repeatedly humbled by the amazing projects happening in the world, I have noticed a change (or rather a reinforcement) in my views. Having spoken to people putting this stuff in action, I've found myself becoming more and more removed and indifferent to much of the political debate and media fanfare surrounding political parties and elections. Having researched for this book, I now find it almost irrelevant to vote for red or blue, left or right, this or that. Of course, I know this is important, but far far more important than this, is to create an entirely new system. To change the base code on which our societies run. To stand firmly in what we think is right, and what are our human rights, and to use technology as the tool to make this a reality.

Because we have been gifted the internet (thanks Tim). Because we now have an evolutionary context which can serve as a platform for us to build the deepest form of democracy the world has ever seen, and one which can serve generations to come as it evolves with them and is written by them. Because government of the people by the people is now a technical possibility. And because we now have cases that show we no longer need to work within the existing system but we can operate according to entirely new principles, principles which allow us to be free, which promote equality, which allow for expression.

As we've touched upon, the future of the internet is on a knife's edge and I think it's our responsibility to keep it safe and nurture it as a living system, just as we would a shared garden, or we should our global environmental ecosystem. I belief this to be a more useful perspective to take.

At a recent talk I described the internet as a 'spiritual technology'. It enables everything and everyone to be interconnected. It allows me to manifest my vision and see it gain mass and increase its gravitational pull until it becomes real. It makes tangible the philosophical idea of humanity being one. It allows for the universal law of perpetual change to be visible and editable by all. It allows for the entire human race to operate from a space of togetherness.

The stories we have read show us that revolution can come by creating genuine alternatives to the existing system. Revolution doesn't have to be about blowing stuff up but rather about building the new. If citizens from every country were to use tools like the ones we've covered here, there would be very little politicians could do to ignore the will of the people. The people's voice will always resonate louder, and we now have the systems we need for those voices to turn into action.

I hope this book awakens the revolutionary in you, I hope it shows the potential for change, I hope it leads to tangible action, to enlightened discussion, but more than anything, I hope it leads to hope. I hope it leads to hope in a better, fairer, more democratic and liberated world so our humanity can thrive.

Be well and happy,
Jon

thanks

Special thanks go to

To Kasper Korjus, Santiago Siri, Adam Jacoby, Colin Megill and Finnur Magnusson for their inspiring work and their kindness in offering me their time and more. Also to John Buck, Hjalmar Gabrielsson and Jeremy Malcolm for deepening my perspective on important fundamentals of this book. To Bruno Marion for his kindness, generosity, experience and support. To Joao Lauro Fonte from bringing some Latin American revolutionary flare to the front cover. To Joakim Jardenberg and Triin Jassov for being wonderful friends and nodes in a beautiful network. To Airbnb and Lost Campers for some homes and offices with lovely views during the writing process.

Personal thanks go to

Franck Dugas for teaching me to walk my own path. To my Mum, Nan and Sis for being so supportive. To Ellie Westbrook for using her energy as a permission slip for my own passion. To Koen Thewissen for believing in me and never providing a problem without a solution. To George Clipp for opening my eyes to much of the world. To Jack Hubbard, my Alpine Guru for being a relentlessly inspiring bigger brother.

And last but not least

Thanks to Jimbo for putting up with my ups and downs, passion and pain, confusion and clarity. Thanks for your big brain, relentless optimism, contagious curiosity and above everything, your free-spirited friendship. I'm lucky to have you pal.

the times they are a-changing

In 1964 Bob Dylan wrote this song to give voice to the sentiments of a disillusioned and underrepresented majority. He created an anthem for a generation of civil rights activists, feminists, gay rights campaigners, environmentalists, free speech advocates, anti-war protesters, anti-nuclear activists, hippies, sexual revolutionaries, and educational reformers.

We can add digital activists to that list. We are a new generation of revolutionaries. Ready to dismantle the dominant power structures and replace them with fair, free, and democratic alternatives. Dylan's words have never felt so relevant:

Come gather around people
Wherever you roam
And admit that the waters
Around you have grown
And accept it that soon
You'll be drenched to the bone
And if your breath to you is worth saving

Then you better start swimming or you'll sink like a
stone
For the times they are a-changing

Come writers and critics
Who prophesize with your pen
And keep your eyes wide
The chance won't come again
And don't speak too soon
For the wheel's still in spin
And there's no telling who that it's naming
For the loser now will be later to win
Cause the times they are a-changing

Come senators, congressmen
Please heed the call
Don't stand in the doorway
Don't block up the hall
For he that gets hurt
Will be he who has stalled
There's the battle outside raging
It'll soon shake your windows and rattle your walls
For the times they are a-changing

Come mothers and fathers
Throughout the land
And don't criticize

What you can't understand
Your sons and your daughters
Are beyond your command
Your old road is rapidly aging
Please get out of the new one if you can't lend your
hand
Cause the times they are a-changing

The line it is drawn
The curse it is cast
The slowest now
Will later be fast
As the present now
Will later be past
The order is rapidly fading
And the first one now will later be last
Cause the times they are a-changing

- The Times They Are A-Changin' by Bob Dylan

a massive gap...

There are no women in this book!

And that's awful! I reached out to a few women in this space doing great things but none were available to share their stories. Only because of busy schedules, nothing else. Changing the world is a 24/7 job.

I wondered whether to hold back on publishing this until I had several female perspectives but to not slow things down and to practice the message of speed we've touched upon, I decided to go ahead with this first edition.

If there is a second, updated edition and any other formats (I've thought of making this a wiki) I will make it a priority to integrate other perspectives and opinions from more diverse backgrounds. I tried, but it just didn't come as easily as I hoped. To get in touch, please email *jon@flux.am*

Lightning Source UK Ltd.
Milton Keynes UK
UKHW02f2016040518

322147UK00010B/649/P

9 781366 778291